Jonathen Brierley

From Philistia

Essays on Church And World

Jonathen Brierley

From Philistia
Essays on Church And World

ISBN/EAN: 9783744724845

Printed in Europe, USA, Canada, Australia, Japan

Cover: Foto ©Thomas Meinert / pixelio.de

More available books at **www.hansebooks.com**

FROM PHILISTIA

ESSAYS ON

CHURCH AND WORLD.

BY

J. BRIERLEY, B.A.

La Vérité étant un sommet, tout chemin qui monte, y conduit.

London:

JAMES CLARKE & CO., 13 & 14, FLEET STREET.

1893.

PREFACE.

THE essayist, of whatsoever degree or pretension, may claim his privileges. One of these,
if regard be had to the best known precedents,
is a happy independence of either historical
or logical sequence in the arrangement of
his topics. Nobody criticises Montaigne, the
father of the tribe, for making a disquisition
on Odours to precede his treatise on Raimond
of Sebonde, or asks why Lord Bacon should
choose that the essay on " Unity in Religion "
be followed by one on the subject of Revenge.
The rule, in fact, in this Bohemian region of
literature, seems to be that the dwellers therein
are free, at a given moment, to think to any
one of the thirty-two points of the compass,
provided only that their thinking be to purpose.

The present writer has availed himself to the
full of the liberty thus accorded to the forth-

putters of *obiter dicta* of all ranks. What
follows in this volume is a collection of scattered
studies, the result of varying moods, circumstances, and mental preoccupations, whose only
link of connection may be said to be their
individuality of standpoint and general drift of
purpose.

From a literary point of view, they will
possibly, with a not uninfluential class of
critics, be regarded as suffering from two
serious disqualifications. The first is the
possession, on the part of the writer, of a
positive religious faith, which he does not, indeed, dogmatically obtrude, but is nevertheless
at no pains to conceal. In criticism, especially
where it touches theology, nothing better fits
the fashion of the hour than that attitude of
religious detachment of which, in our day,
Renan and Edmond Schérer have given such
brilliant examples. The assumption of it
enables the writer to treat the differing faiths
somewhat as imperial Rome dealt with the
religions brought under her sway, with the
toleration, namely, and patronage which a
superior and governing class feels it can afford
to extend to inferior and subject races. It is a
literary manner full of possibilities for effective

posing. Its capabilities must, however, be sought elsewhere than in these pages.

That is not the worst. What is here written will be found, not only definitely related to religious faith, but to a form of it which polite society has, with impressive unanimity, pronounced upon. These essays are dated from the heart of Philistia. In other words, their author belongs to that region of *esprits bornés*, and of intellectual density, connoted by the terms Protestant Nonconformist. To enter here will be doubtless, to many cultured persons, an adventure as serious and unwonted as to traverse the realm of

> Antres vast and deserts idle,
> Of anthropophagi and men whose heads
> Do grow beneath their shoulders.

If any such make the venture we can only wish them a safe and happy issue out of it. Should they emerge alive it may, perhaps, be with the tidings that the tales of intellectual savagery in vogue concerning its inhabitants owe, like some of Othello's stories, a good deal to the imagination of their authors.

It remains to be said that the acknowledgments of the author are due to Mr. John

Murray, to the Editor of the "Sun" Magazine, to the Rev. J. G. Rogers, and to Messrs. James Clarke and Co., for permission to make use, in this volume, of articles that have previously appeared in publications with which they are, or have been, connected.

London, May, 1893.

CONTENTS.

CHURCH AND WORLD.

RABELAIS.

In the debt which the nineteenth century owes to the sixteenth there are some outstanding accounts which do not seem as yet to have been precisely stated. And assuredly one of the largest of these is that under the name of Francis Rabelais. He is one of a trio of men who, born within a year or two of each other, not only moulded their own century, but live in every pulse of ours. With two of these we have no great difficulty as to the appraisement. Luther stands in our minds for Protestantism and all that it contains. Ignatius Loyola represents the genius of Catholicism and the reassertion of the principle of authority in religion. But the third of our trio, the Frenchman, can we fit him into a formula as easily as the German and the Spaniard? And yet he is to be reckoned with. He is one of the

1

creators of the modern spirit, and his force, so
far from being spent, is a tide steadily rising.
Any one who considers the present free-trade
in literature and ideas, the way in which the
inner life and thought of different peoples is
mingling and inter-penetrating, and who then
studies the influence which Rabelais has
exerted on one of the most important of these
peoples and literatures, will recognise in him a
power for good or ill not inferior to that of the
commanding spirits whose names we have
placed beside his own. No man, it is safe to
affirm, is more distinctly responsible for the
France of to-day. Not only may we say, with
Châteaubriand, that he is the father of French
literature, but that he is, in a way, the father
of the French character. For the makers of
France who have come after him, both the
thinkers and the actors, have all worked with
the consciousness of this man behind them. It
is not the extent to which succeeding writers
have quoted him or drawn on his materials.
It is that he created for his countrymen an
atmosphere, a medium through which they saw
things. At a critical period in the history of
civilisation, when men's views and feelings on
the most vital subjects were in a state of fusion
waiting for fresh moulds in which to run,
Rabelais struck in and made one. It was not
Calvin's or Luther's or Loyola's. That it was

so far away from theirs has made all the difference to the modern world. We propose in this
sketch to try and find out what kind of a mould
it was—in other words, to trace out some of the
bearings of Rabelais' influence on the life of
to-day.

It is here, however, that our difficulties begin.
Rabelais is, *par excellence*, the stone of stumbling for hasty generalisers. How tempting,
for instance, for the phrase-monger to sum
him up as representing the pagan side of the
Renaissance! The definition will do, provided
you keep your eye turned steadily away from
one whole half of the man. He has been
compared with Lucian; and it is easy, if we
want to, to multiply resemblances between
them. Like the great second-century writer,
Rabelais had absorbed all the learning of his
time. Like him he made the object of his
raillery not only the established religion, but
also the philosophies most in vogue. And the
dubious attitude of Lucian towards Christianity,
the new religion which was replacing the official
paganism of the empire, might be compared
with Rabelais' relation to the reformed faith.
But we should utterly mistake the author of
Pantagruel if we simply made him a second
edition of the old world Pyrrhonist who wrote
the "Hermotimus" and "Dialogues of the
Gods." A still greater blunder would be to

take him, as some of the older commentators
have done, altogether *au sérieux :* to regard him
as " a man with a mission," who had set himself definitely to destroy certain things in the
world, and to build up others, whose *contes
gras* and wild buffooneries concealed grave
meanings which it behoved the critic to search
out and expound. It is, in fact, no use approach-
ing him with hypotheses or endeavouring to fit
him into definitions.   He is his own definition :
Rabelais is Rabelais.   He has put his whole
self into his work, and that self is a marvellously
mixed one.   Dr. Jekyll and Mr. Hyde are both
there.   " He will be the enigma of posterity,"
wrote Pierre Boulanger of him after his death,
and the prediction has been verified.   A book
could be filled with the contradictory opinions
formed of him by the ablest men from Montaigne downwards. Victor Hugo's line is hardly
an exaggeration :

"Rabelais qui nul ne comprit."

Instead, then, of beginning by labelling him
with a phrase, let us rather study some of his
many sides and allow our theory of him, if
theory there must be, to grow instead of being
made.

First, what does he count for in the purely
intellectual side of the sixteenth-century movement?

There is one thing in which all who have studied him are agreed, and that is the encyclopædic character of his attainments. When Panurge was first encountered by Pantagruel he replied to his inquiries in thirteen different languages. They were all of them tongues with which the author was conversant. He was a master of Hebrew, Arabic, Greek, Latin, Italian, Spanish, German. The Greek and Latin literatures were at his fingers' ends. He was profoundly versed in law and in philosophy. Though he despised astrology and the black arts, no man was more familiar with their lore. He was acknowledged as one of the first authorities of his day in medicine and in botany. In his quotations and allusions, whether it be a question of the Hebrew casuists, or of some obscure commentator on Aristotle, of Arab doctors, of Neoplatonist speculation, or of the disputed questions of the Schools, he is never caught tripping.

Perhaps one of the most striking signs of his presence in the sixteenth century as an intellectual force is the mark he has left on the French language. He may be said to have presided at the birth of his native tongue as an instrument of literature. Up to his day the learned world everywhere regarded Latin as the only respectable medium of ideas. Rabelais showed to Europe what could be done with his

native French. But he dealt with it not as its
servant, but as its master. In order that its
previously somewhat thin stream might carry
the deeply laden bark of his learning and
imagination, he found he must both broaden
and deepen it. And he plies his task like one
of those steam navvies which nowadays cut
through isthmuses and hew out ship-canals.
We doubt if a writer could be named in any
literature who wrought such structural changes
and introduced such quantities of new elements
into a language as did he.

Coming from the language to the matter of
his works, it is impossible to pass their threshold
without noticing the extraordinary licence
he permits himself, a licence frequently
amounting to an obscenity which repels and
disgusts. " You may wash him," says
Thackeray somewhere, "and scrub him to your
heart's content, but you will never get him
clean." It is true. His work is certainly not
virginibus puerisque. A Bowdlerised Rabelais
would be no Rabelais at all. That he had any
idea himself of outraging decency or morality
in this is not in the least probable. It was the
manner of his age. It was a time which saw
no irregularity in a Margaret of Navarre writing
books of mystical devotion and the Heptameron.
Hutten's "Litteræ Obscurorum Virorum," the
book which has been called the egg out of

which Luther hatched the Reformation, contains stories as gross as any which Panurge recounts. The fiercest opponents of Rabelais in his own day did not fasten on these things as the objectionable matter. Had he not attacked the Sorbonne and the Papacy, his Catholic readers would have found here no ground of offence. Calvin only began to denounce him when his earlier leanings to Protestantism had disappeared.

To reach the summit to which the Rabelaisian pathway leads means, then, a good deal of wading through the mire. We have, as Saint-Beuve says, to take long leaps if we would avoid the muddy places. But when there, the outlook is marvellously extensive, and across some of the richest tracts of country. Let us take a glance or two.

No question touches the modern world more closely than that of education. We are eager for light not only in schools and colleges, but also as to private culture. We have lists drawn out of "The hundred best books," and we read eagerly what distinguished men have to say on "Books that have influenced me."

Our author had his ideas on culture, which the nineteenth century may still have something to learn from. Let us see what he regarded as the true idea of a liberal education. We get a good specimen of it in the letter of Gargantua to his son Pantagruel, in Book 2: "I desire that you learn the languages perfectly. First the Greek, as Quintilian advises, and then the Latin. After that, Hebrew, for the Holy Scripture, as well as Chaldee and Arabic. In Greek, form your style on Plato; in Latin, on Cicero. Of the liberal arts, as geometry, arithmetic, and music, I gave you some taste while you were young, five or six years ago. Follow them up, and especially astronomy. Let astrology alone, as vain and useless. Of civil law I want you to learn by heart the best texts, and to compare them with philosophy. I want you also to give yourself specially to the study of the facts of nature, so that there be no sea, river, fountain, of which you do not know the fishes, and that you may know also the birds of the air, all trees. . . . all the metals and precious stones. Study carefully the medical works of the Greeks, Romans, and Arabs, without despising the Talmudists and Cabalists; and by frequent anatomical practice acquire knowledge of that other world—viz., man. And for a certain time each day study the Holy Scriptures, first, in Greek, the New Testament and epistles of the Apostles, and then, in Hebrew, the Old Testament." This programme represents, we imagine, pretty accurately the line of study pursued by Rabelais himself in the fifteen years

he spent as a Cordelier at Fontenoy. Lest,
however, we should suppose that our philosopher
regarded a limitless course of reading as com-
prehending the whole of education, we may
turn to his history of Gargantua in Book 1, and
study the plan laid down for him by his tutor
Ponocrates. We find there seven pages out of
ten taken up with a description of his gymnastic
exercises, and the general training and care of
the body. It is singular that his countrymen
have in this respect so egregiously failed to
catch the spirit of their master. The French
youth at school and college knows next to
nothing of outdoor sports as we understand
them. Education with him is a constant drive
of the brain. What exercise he gets is
grudgingly allowed in just sufficient quantity to
keep his body going. If in this respect they
had taken to heart the lessons of their mentor,
and had taught their young people, as
Gargantua was taught, to swim, to run, to
ride, to hunt, to handle arms, and to live in the
open, we should not now be hearing so many
complaints of their physical degeneracy. But
Rabelais has not finished when he has drilled
body and brain. At the end of the letter from
Gargantua, from which we have already quoted,
we have his view of the moral side of the
question. "But since, as Solomon says, wisdom
enters not into an evil mind, and knowledge

without conscience is only the ruin of the soul; therefore serve, love, and fear God, and in Him place all thy thoughts and all thy hope; and be joined to Him by faith which works by love. . . . Give not thy heart to vanity, for this life is transitory, but the Word of God abideth for ever. Be serviceable to thy neighbours, and love them as thyself. Revere thy teachers, flee the company of men whom you do not wish to resemble, and receive not the grace of God in vain."

After three centuries of theory and experiment in education it is to be doubted if we have got hold of anything better than this.

If these were his intellectual ideals, what were his political and social ones?

His theory of government was evidently that which Lord Beaconsfield more than once hinted at—that of a sage and capable monarch who sums up in himself, and gives expression to, the collective opinion and feeling of his people. His three giants, Grandgousier, Gargantua, and Pantagruel, are all model kings—wise, affable, peaceful, detesting war for its own sake, but capable when attacked of defending themselves and their subjects.

Could anything be more admirable as a picture of the attitude of a true governor under difficult circumstances than that of Grandgousier when attacked by the fire-eating Picro-

chole ? Though conscious of vastly superior
strength, yet, hating the ravages of war, he
sends embassy after embassy to his hostile
neighbour in order to bring him to reason and
to keep the peace. He drops sentences here
worthy to be written in letters of gold in the
cabinets of kings : " We call that brigandage
and wickedness which the Saracens and bar-
barians of former days called prowess." " The
imitation of the Alexanders, the Hercules, the
Hannibals, the Scipios, the Cæsars, and such
like, we regard as contrary to the profession of
the Gospel, by which we are commanded to
keep, rule and administer each one his country
and territory, and not hostilely to invade those
of others."

It is impossible, in fact, to study Rabelais
anywhere in his views on government and
political policy without recognising a spirit
truly generous and humane, a man who hated
oppression, and who believed that power was a
trust to be employed in making one's fellow-
men happier and better.

At the same time his instincts were aristo-
cratic. He believed in an aristos of position
and ability. On the subject of a representative
government he makes Pantagruel express himself thus. It is in his adjudication on the
famous case of Baisecul v. Homvesne. " In all
companies there are more fools than wise men,

and it is the majority usually that carries the
day." The sentence itself is a quotation from
Livy, but it would have been beautifully appropriate in the mouth of Thomas Carlyle. The
Curé of Meudon and the Sage of Chelsea were
very much at one, methinks, on the subject of
the democracy.

It is impossible in a study of Rabelais to pass
by his treatment of women. His want of
respect for the sex is a radical defect of his
work. He is false here to the Renaissance
spirit. In Italy it had idolised woman. Dante
and Petrarch consecrated to her their loftiest
poetry, while Raphael and Michel Angelo made
her features shine with a mystic, celestial
beauty. In the sphere of Protestantism, Luther,
in his public teaching and in his own home,
treated woman with serious and Christian
respect: a sentiment echoed by Erasmus in his
treatise on Christian marriage. Rabelais'
heresy in this respect must be ascribed to his
early associations and to his monkish training.
We never hear of his mother, and she probably
had died before exercising any influence over
him. To the monkish orders, with their vows
of celibacy and chastity, woman represented
the greatest of temptations, the shortest road,
in fact, to the bottomless pit. And when, as
in the time of Rabelais, these strict rules had
produced a reaction in favour of unbridled

licence, the conception of woman remained the same. The demoralised monk in pursuit of sensual enjoyment thought of his partner only as an instrument of his pleasures, and, when conscience pricked him, as the occasion of his downfall.

To one who, like Rabelais, had passed through such a training it would have been like jumping off his own shadow to have thought of woman as a teacher and an inspirer, as one who could be intellectually or spiritually a helper to man. Hence all through his work, knowledge, virtue, nobleness of character, are embodied in his men. Woman is the butt of his ridicule, the object of his coarsest stories. It is a capital fault, the influence of which has been disastrous on his countrymen. Had France possessed from the beginning of her literature, instead of the Rabelaisian idea, the image of a noble womanhood, helping man towards his loftiest ideals, the history of her literature and of her people might have been different.

The attitude of Rabelais towards the great religious questions of his day is an interesting study. We see clearly that his differences with the leaders in the mighty strife that was then being waged were not so much an affair of doctrines as of temperament. And his temperament was one which, while sufficiently

comprehensible to the nineteenth century, was
absolutely unintelligible to the sixteenth. The
chiefs of the Reformation as well as the
Catholic doctors of the Sorbonne, alike regarded
him as a deadly enemy. Neither party could
understand a man who refused to take sides;
who, while merciless to the abuses and weak
points of Romanist theory and practice, was
equally unsparing to the party of Geneva.
Both, in their fierce resentment and despair of
making the man out, took refuge in what
seemed to them the only remaining hypothesis
—viz., that he was an atheist and an enemy of
all religion.

No conclusion could be more absurd. It
would be difficult to point to any works of our
own time in the department of imaginative
literature so saturated as are those of Rabelais
with religious principle, so definitely recognising the presence of the living God in human
affairs.

Much of his work showed what seemed a
distinctly Protestant leaning. To abuse the
Pope, to trounce the monks, to pour ridicule on
the Sorbonne and all its works, while at the
same time testifying everywhere, as he does, to
a hearty belief in God, to a reverence for Scripture and especially for the New Testament and
the writings of St. Paul, all this one would
think would be enough to stamp him as on this

side of the great controversy. And yet he was no Protestant. Between him and the Reformation leaders was a great gulf fixed. Calvin and he were at open war. In his fourth Book he denounces the "demoniacal Calvin" "the impostor of Geneva"; while, on his side, the Reformer expressed himself with equal bitterness.

It was impossible for two men so profoundly different in temper to appreciate or even understand each other. Calvin was a man who knew nothing of compromises, who believed that truth, purity, salvation were on the side he fought for, and that on the other were only superstition, errors, and corruption.

It is the heroic temper which makes history; but the equilibrium of things seems to demand also spirits of a different mould. Rabelais had in him nothing of the partisan. He was gifted with the embarrassing faculty of seeing two sides of a question. For one thing, the austerity of Geneva revolted his joyous temper; and for another, he had no desire to share the fate of his friend Etienne Dolet, and get burned as a heretic. But that is not all. When we talk of the Reformation we must never forget the great Reform movement which took place in Catholicism itself in the sixteenth century.

In fact, from the beginning of the Renaissance, up to and beyond Luther's time, the

abuses of Rome had been as fiercely attacked
by Catholics who lived and died within her pale
as by the leaders of Protestantism. That party
of Reform had Dante as its poet, Erasmus for
its scholar, Gerson for its theologian and
mystic, Michel Angelo for its artist, and
Catherine of Sienna for its saint. The
Cardinals who surrounded Paul III., such as
Contarini and Caraffa, had elaborated a
doctine of justification by faith which it is
difficult to distinguish from that of Luther,
and which was preached with passionate
fervour throughout the length and breadth
of Italy. Rabelais defies classification; but
if he is to be put anywhere in the matter of
ecclesiastical relations, it is by the side of this
party. His contention, so far as he entered
into controversy, was not so much against the
Catholic Church as against Ultramontanism.
He was in this respect an ancestor of Bossuet
and one of the founders of Gallicanism.

But we should not understand Rabelais or
his influence if we discussed him simply in
relation to controversies of this kind. It is as
a great humanist, with an outlook and a
philosophy of life all his own, that he counts
as so unique a force in literature and in the
evolution of modern life. No man, at least, no
modern man, has been so startlingly frank. He
has no concealments, no reserves. He has no

closet in which to lock up his skeletons. He
lets all his nature speak. The animal in him
was strong and masterful. All through his
pages rings the note of a rude physical force
which has no notion of being repressed or put
down. His characteristic may, in fact, be said
to be an enormous appetite in all directions.
His intellect was voracious, and so was his
stomach. To feed his mind the whole world of
knowledge was not too much. But he wanted
a larder and a wine-cellar on the same scale as
the library. To the ascetic doctrine he replied
by a " no " so mighty that its echoes have been
ringing through literature ever since.

His ultimate views of life may perhaps be
described as a fusion of the Greek idea with
Christianity. To understand him we need
certainly to take note of the pagan side of the
Renaissance. In Italy especially, with which
Rabelais was so well acquainted, it had produced as its first effect a profound scepticism
and an utter licence of manners. Not only had
Scholasticism been cast aside, but practically
Christianity also. Aristophanes and Anacreon,
rather than Paul and the Fathers, supplied the
Italy of the latter half of the fifteenth century
with its views of life. It was beyond the Alps,
with Reuchlin, Melancthon and Luther, that
the Revival of letters resulted in a purified
Christianity.

The peculiarity of Rabelais' position is that
he drank deeply of the two streams, and that
his temperament tended to assimilate them
both. His was a nature gifted with a " rire
enorme," to use Victor Hugo's phrase, and his
whole conception of the universe had to fit in
to that. He could not understand Christianity
as the Reformers understood it, simply because
he had no capacity for the serious or the awful.
That side of religion which appealed to his
sense of justice, to his sympathy, to his gener-
osity, he freely accepted. The rest passed over
him. God was to him a benevolent and gracious
Providence, to whom he owed the blessings he
enjoyed. He bowed reverently before Christ
as the expression of suffering and self-sacrificing
love.

But he must have room for his laugh. What
could Geneva do with a man who treated hell,
in the manner of Lucian, as a place where the
actors play parts as ridiculous as those of a
Christmas pantomime?

His summing up of life is that all is vanity,
but that the mistake is to groan about it. Life
is a burlesque. We are all fools and the solemn
fool is the biggest of all. Pantagruelism is a
" certaine gayeté d'esprit conficte en mepris des
choses fortuites." The sentence he puts into
the mouth of his ideal character Pantagruel
expresses perhaps better than any other his

habitual attitude of mind: "For all the goods which the sky covers and that earth contains. . . . are not worthy to move our affections or to trouble our mind and spirit."

This bold eclecticism of culture, this easy mixture of inspiration from Palestine and from Greece is the special note of Rabelais, and it has become the note of a large portion of the modern world.

THE NEW HELLENISM.

In these easy-going days we experience no great astonishment in witnessing the appearance among us of the most fantastic cults. We hear of an English barrister who has become an enthusiastic follower of Mohammed, and of an American Colonel who proposes to convert us to Buddhism. Both will be tolerated, but we doubt if either will succeed in attracting much of a following amongst the English public. There is another religion, however, which is much more likely to become fashionable, and which has indeed already considerable vogue in certain circles. It is the cult which places before us the old Greek idea of life as the only true one, and moans over the last eighteen hundred years of Western history as a long and grievous aberration from it.

The idea, to be sure, is not new, though, as we shall see directly, it has in our day taken a more definite and dogmatically assertive form. It is not new, we say. The Renaissance, on one side of it, at least, was a move towards

Hellenism. If, in art, we compare the pictures of Rubens, of Titien, of Paul Veronese with those of distinctly Catholic painters like Van Eyck or Fra Angelico, we see into what a different, into what a Pagan world we have come. Even their so-called sacred paintings have no really religious inspiration, while the bulk of their works are pagan in subject. In literature, Rabelais, Boccaccio, and Ariosto, to say nothing of writers like Aretino, are frankly at issue with the Catholic dogma and morality. The French Revolution witnessed another revival of the Hellenic idea. Its republicanism, its theory both of public and private life, boasted of being Greek and classic. In the early part of this century, Byron and Keats, on the one hand, were strongly tinctured with this spirit, and Mr. Swinburne is to-day its fervid representative. It is in France again, however, that the cult has received its latest and most striking development. Victor Hugo has chanted its praise in the "Légende des Siècles," while M. Sully Prudhomme, one of the most original and profound of French contemporary poets, gives us the line—

> Bienheureuse la destinée
> D'un enfant grec du monde ancien.

The full development of the idea, however, has been reserved for a woman. Mme. Adam,

in a series of interesting romances, of which
" Paienne," " Grecque," and " Laïde," are the
best known, has with passionate fervour and
without the slightest reserve, preached the new
religion. Her creed is the love and the following of nature, the full enjoyment of the seen
and the present, the complete deliverance from
" other-worldliness," the only law recognised
being the preservation of all the passions and
faculties in their mutual harmony. This she
imagines to have been the Greek idea, which
Christianity has done so much to spoil. The
Western world has suffered for nigh 2,000
years from the injection into it of the Semitic
virus, and is only beginning to recover from it.
She believes in the South, in its bright sun-
shine and its warmth of passion. The North is to
be distrusted. It is the region of cold-blooded-
ness, of mysticism, of gloomy theologies. When
Mme. Adam discusses the relation of Christianity to woman, she becomes almost lyric in
her passion. " Would you have," says she in
" Jean et Pascal," " my entire opinion? The
irreconcilable enemy of Christianity ought to
be woman. All the suspicions, all the insults,
all the hatreds of its doctrine are levelled
against her. Woman is the great temptation,
the principal aid of the devil. The love she
inspires is the crowning iniquity. We shall
only be happy when we have got rid of this

nightmare, and have returned to that line of development which man, 2,300 years ago, was pursuing by the shores of the Ægean Sea."

All this is very interesting, and would be important, if it were true. Indeed, we must, any way, confess to its importance, since it is the note of a school which has many disciples, and is exercising an ever-widening influence on the mind of to-day. But will these ideas bear examination? We strongly suspect, to begin with, that the New Græcism will turn out, as a French critic has put it, to be a great deal more new than Greek. It is astonishing how people, when possessed by an idea, will allow it to carry them in a direction clean contrary to the facts of the case. When so distinguished a writer, for instance, as M. Renan finds in the Athenian populace "a people of aristocrats, an entire public composed of connoisseurs, a democracy which had seized the requirements of art in a manner which the most cultured among us fail to do," is he not giving us a fancy picture? The Athenian populace, as drawn for us from the life by Aristophanes, suggests to us anything but this idea. But even if it were true, there is one element of the situation omitted from M. Renan's account, but which we cannot afford to ignore. The Greek citizenship was based upon slavery. Aristotle frankly tells us that in an ideal republic no one who works with his hands can be admitted as a citizen.

But is this system—that of a privileged order which shall win ease and luxury by laying all its burdens upon an inferior and enslaved caste—that which our Hellenists propose for us in the nineteenth century?

What, too, should we make of the "patriotism," so called, of the Greek republic, consisting, as it did, of a religious hatred of all outside their own city, a few square miles of territory? "Let the citizens," says Æschylus in the *Choephori*, "be full of love to each other, and of a common hatred towards the enemy." We have imagined that the modern spirit which is breaking down the barriers between races, and proclaiming the solidarity and brotherhood of mankind, was really an advance upon this. But we may have been mistaken.

What a strange notion, too, to one who has a real acquaintance with Greek literature, to suppose that its inner life, as compared with the life of Christendom, was marked by special joyousness and felicity! When we listen to the authorised exponents of that life, what do we find? Was the *Agamemnon* of Æschylus or the *Œdipus Tyrannus* of Sophocles, or the *Medea* of Euripides, the outcome of minds which possessed a sunnier view of life than our own? On the contrary, can anything be more sombre than the conceptions which run through all of them, of a fate which pushes men to their ruin, of fierce passions which hurry them into the commission of terrible crimes—crimes which bring upon them the avenging furies to dog hereafter their flying steps?

What provision had the Greeks in the way of consolation for old age and the prospect of death? Let us hear Anacreon, the poet who celebrated every form of sensuous enjoyment. "My temples are blanched already. My hair is white. I am no longer young. It is on this account I groan, for I fear Tartarus, and the abyss of Hades is horrible. The descent to it is frightful, and once there, there is no return."

This is not particularly cheering. Let us add to it the words of the chorus in *Œdipus at Colona* :—"The best thing is never to be born. The next best, to die as soon as possible. For hardly has youth brought its follies, but what pains, what misfortunes fall upon us! And at the end comes old age, chagrined, powerless, unsociable, exacting, in which all evils are united."

Where are we to look for the Greek joyousness? Be it remembered, too, that a return to this ideal time would mean a crippling of our intellectual liberty. Tastes differ, but the majority of us would hardly care to go back to a condition in which, if we spoke our exact

mind, we should run the risk of sharing
Socrates' bowl of hemlock.

But woman, we are told, is the martyr of the
Christian system, and it is she acccordingly
who ought to lead the revolt against it in
favour of Greek Naturalism. The indictment
we have quoted from Mme. Adam is a heavy
one, and at first sight there may be something
to bear it out.

There have been Christian teachers and
Christian systems of theology, that have dealt
with woman in very much the fashion which
our lady Hellenist stigmatises. But this teaching was not of the essence of Christianity. It
was the teaching of Monasticism, and of those
Latin fathers who so largely misrepresented the
primitive church doctrine. Woman in modern
civilisation does not come out so badly as a
product of the Christian system, when we see
her taking her place in the van of every movement, and sharing to the full in the latest
developments of life and thought. Supposing
that, in exchange for all this, she went back to
her position in the Greek republics. She
would find it one in which the idea of love
was reduced to its coarsest elements, in which
the union of the sexes, instead of being one
which comprehended the whole nature, and gave
fullest scope to her faculty of moral inspiration, was regarded purely on its animal side.

As to the amount of respect she might look for, let us judge of it from the treatment she receives in the literature which represents Hellenic life and thought at its highest level. Let any one read the *Seven against Thebes* of Æschylus, or the *Ajax* of Sophocles, or any one of the comedies of Aristophanes, simply for their teaching on this point. It is evident they are written by men to whom the intellectual and moral rank now enjoyed by women in Christendom were impossible ideas. In the *Seven against Thebes*, for example, Eteocles speaks of woman as the "Sex detested of the wise"; as a being "insupportable from her pride after a victory, but whose terror during a battle brings disaster to the family and to the state." Farther on, he breaks out with, "The women! What a race!"

In the *Ajax*, when Tecmessa seeks to console her lord in his misfortunes, and lead him to abandon his desperate projects, he treats her with the haughtiest disdain, as one whose words are unworthy of serious notice. Would Mme. Adam and her feminine admirers care to become Greek at this price?

Moreover, to the loss of public and private respect would be added that of the modern woman's notion of comfort. She would have no home in our sense of the word. The Greek life did not contain the idea. It was an out-of-door existence, splendid enough on its public side, but from which our domestic pleasures were entirely absent.

The truth is, the school of the new Hellenism has been nourishing itself on dreams. The world it paints for us has never existed. It is as far from the actual fact as was Rousseau's dream of savagery as the ideal human existence. It is easy to understand how it has arisen. Man's quarrel with the actual takes ever and anon the form of a reversion to earlier types of life as more perfect than the existing one. In this case, a wealthy, luxurious, and highly sceptical society, in search of a respectable title for its philosophy of life, has hit upon this of Greek naturalism. In its revolt against Christianity, and in its anxiety to obtain some sanction for its sensuous tendencies, it labours to show that the system which at present restrains its licence is inferior. To this end it paints for us the picture of a people and an age outside of Christianity, whom it represents as enjoying a higher and happier existence than our own. We have seen what value there is in this contention.

When stripped of its present Greek ornaments, and reduced to its own proper merits, the new cult does not somehow greatly inspire us. We are not likely, so long as our minds keep healthy, to prefer a creed which offers luxury to the few at the expense of the many, to that which sets us to work for the good of all.

And were we even of the favoured few to whom its offered enjoyments would be possible, we know we should not be satisfied with them. In a world where, no matter what our social position, we are in presence of such realities as physical pain and inward anguish, where our social circle is ever liable to be torn by bereavement, and where, across our own pathway, death digs his yawning trench, we need something more for our inward strengthening than a cult of æsthetic beauty or of sensuous pleasure.

Christianity can very easily assimilate all that is really valuable in the Greek idea. But we cannot afford that it shall abdicate in favour of it. Not till we are prepared to give up the highest in thought and feeling that the human race has yet come into possession of, till we have cast out the idea of duty, and the grace of service, till we have become blunted to the exquisite joy which faith brings, can we admit that the Christian religion has been other than the most potent instrument of human progress, or be anxious to desert its standard for that of other leaders.

ST. AUGUSTINE IN LITERATURE.

In this year of grace our title seems almost an anachronism. For what, in 1893, does Augustine count for in literature? In an age in which people expect to have everything boiled down for them to a three or four line paragraph, what chance has a man of being listened to who comes to us with more than a hundred volumes, written in the Latin tongue, on subjects the most abstruse; and who, moreover, speaks across the distance of fourteen centuries? As a matter of fact, to most of us Augustine is a name and nothing more. The average English Christian has some vague notions about the "Confessions" and the "City of God" as the works of the African bishop; and he has learned to associate him with certain theological dogmas at present largely discredited. But how little does this represent of the real man! He was a theologian, it is true, but he was so much more. A personality like his is like a vast mountain, whose far-stretching slopes present every variety of scenery. He is a man about whose work and influence a hundred things may be said without apparently diminishing the number of things still left to be said. We will content ourselves in this article with getting a glimpse here and there of aspects of his work the less generally known.

To understand what he has been to the world we need to go back to the Middle Ages. We find him there ruling in all departments as the intellectual king. In philosophy he had left no subject uninvestigated. As a publicist his dicta regulated the government of states and of societies. In morals he had the same supremacy, and in general literature his utterances on a thousand topics affecting the manifold sides of human life were accepted as models of what was most cogent in argument, lofty in inspiration, and moving in eloquence.

And there is this other attraction in his writings. They present us with an almost complete picture of the opinions on all the the great subjects of thought of the ancient world. There is hardly a religious or philosophical idea of antiquity which does not come under his review. The poets and philosophers of Greece and of Rome, the Neoplatonists of Alexandria, the Gnostic sects and Oriental religionists, and thinkers of all shades, as well as the Greek and Latin fathers of the Church who preceded him, are constantly before us in his pages. He is a kind of lens, concentrating in its focus all the scattered rays of the past.

We have spoken of his undisputed reign through long centuries. We wish we could give our readers an idea of how complete that was. To do so we should need to dip into the literature of each separate century as it rolls, and show what he counted for in it. A glance or two in this direction must content us. It is interesting, for instance, in the fifth century to find Cassiodorus, the Emperor Theodoric's great minister, in his retirement in Calabria, making his one occupation the study of our author, and in the eighth to see Alcuin, Charlemagne's literary right - hand man, causing the father's logical treatises to be copied and spread abroad throughout the schools of the Empire. The ninth century shows us J. Scot Erigena, the father of Middle Age Mysticism, whose profound study of the psychological problems of the spiritual life become the basis of the systems of Bernard, of Bonaventura, and of Gerson, first saturating himself with Augustine. As to Bonaventura, it is enough to open his "Itinerary of the Soul Towards God," or his "Seven Roads of Eternity," to recognise everywhere in it the African bishop. And the same may be said of the writings of Anselm and of Bernard.

While thus puissant amongst the schoolmen,
he bulks no less largely with the great spirits
who prepared and inaugurated the Renaissance.
Dante nourished his soul on the " City of
God." Petrarch in writing his treatise on the
" Contempt of the World " imagines Augustine
as his interlocutor. When Boccaccio sent him
Augustine's exposition of the Psalms he
thanked him for it as for " a magnificent
and most splendid present." When the
Reformation came, we have another remarkable illustration of the predominance of
Augustine over two bitterly opposed parties.
All the world knows how the name which
is the corner-stone of Catholic theology is
that also which the founders of Protestantism
most frequently invoked. Luther's work
" De Arbitrio Servo," in which he breaks
a lance with Erasmus is, as he himself
confesses, of the great father's inspiration.
And Calvinism is, of course, Augustinianism
revised.

We could easily push this review of authority
and influence to later times. We could point
out, for instance, what in the seventeenth century
Bossuet and Fenelon, Pascal and the Port
Royalists, Descartes and Malebranche, owed to
him. One could devote an article to illustrate
the way in which philosophers, who have been
specially lauded for the perfect originality of

their ideas, have been, in fact, anticipated in them by Augustine.

Descartes, for instance, has received unmeasured homage for his doctrine of intellectual certitude, as summed up in his famous formula, "Cogito Ergo Sum" ("I think, therefore I am"). But we turn to the "Soliloquies" of Augustine, and we find the very argument, expressed almost in the same words. But a more striking example remains. Schlegel has received much praise for working out, in his "Philosophy of History," the idea of the development of the human race as a whole, presenting the same features, and following the same stages as that of a single individual in his progress from infancy to manhood. This idea, by the way, is again copied by Bishop Temple in his once famous but now almost forgotten contribution to "Essays and Reviews." But we get all this in full detail and with amplest illustration in the "City of God." So difficult is it to find, in the region of ideas, any new thing under the sun.

To attempt to measure the good and the evil in the influence of this great personality would be a difficult task. For it was a mixed influence. The dark shadows of the age in which he lived were in some degree reflected in him, and hence we find his support lent to abuses which the power of his name helped to keep alive for many centuries. Thus, though pleading always for the individual rights of slaves, he gave a kind of support to the institution; he preached the divine right of kings, and what is more deplorable, justified religious persecution by the State. But, turning from these blots on his name, let us think rather on the good he wrought. He worked with all his might to re-establish that idea of the family which Paganism and the corruptions of the later empire had done so much to destroy. He insisted on the rights of children and of women. He proclaims the equality of the wife in relation to her husband. He served the democracy in upholding the dignity of labour as against the contempt which had been cast upon it by antiquity. He protested against torture as an instrument of criminal procedure. If he admits the necessity of war, he declares that its end should be to procure peace, and not conquest. His immortal work, "The City of God," renders him the father of the philosophy of history. It was worthy of this great and unworldly spirit, at a time when all order and justice seemed banished from the world, to offer to men a theory of history which regarded the human movement as under a Divine order, which linked all events in a continuous and disciplined progress, which discerned in its seeming confusions a concealed but all-wise purpose, and which predicted the ultimate and glorious triumph of good.

The throne which Augustine for so long occupied must now be said to be vacant. Neither as theologian, philosopher, or publicist can he be any longer said to be a dictator. The world is not likely in the future again to speak or think pure Augustinianism. The intellectual stream from which we now drink comes from many and widely-divergent sources. But it will for a long time yet retain some of the flavour which he has imparted, and be the better for it. And the world could hardly desire a nobler gift than the work and influence in it of a man who should be to our age what Augustine was to his, one who, supreme among thinkers, and master of all the science of his time, should apply his powers and his acquirements in absolute devotion to the service of faith and to the development of his fellows on their noblest side.

THE DANGEROUS YEARS.

The risks of life on its physical side have been made the subject of exhaustive analyses, whose results appear in the tables of insurance companies. Those results are, as we know, all in favour of youth. A man's chances of surviving an accident, or an epidemic, or a severe winter, are many times more per cent. at 20 than they are at 50. Prudent men are aware of this, and take precautions accordingly. What, however, we do not possess is a study, carried out with the same scientific accuracy, of life's moral risks. We have no actuaries in this department to calculate for us the chances of a breakdown in character between 40 and 50, as compared with those between 20 and 30. That some such analysis is needed is evident, when we examine the curious blunders which are fallen into on this subject by moralists and preachers.

In the average modern pulpit, it is the "young man" who is perpetually being gone for in sermons and lectures. The dangers

which beset the third decade of human existence are set forth with an iteration which
becomes almost wearisome.   This decade is, it
seems, like the *mauvais pas* in an Alpine ascent.
Once across that, without a tumble, and our
guides assure us the rest will be plain sailing.
Let a young man be safely landed in the region
of wedlock and home, and be definitely connected with the religious society to which his
forbears belonged, and he ceases to be a subject
of serious anxiety to his spiritual counsellors.
And so it comes to pass that the "sermon to
young men" is an essential and familiar part
of a preacher's repertory, while the "sermon to
men of forty-five" is the one we never hear of.

It is the assumption contained in all this that
I venture now to call in question.   When the
thing has been looked into, I believe it will be
found that what the actuary finds with reference to man's physical life is precisely what is
true of his moral life.   There is danger enough
for youth and young manhood in its passage
through this difficult world.   But the most
slippery places are further on.

When in support of this contention we set
ourselves to examine history and literature, we
find it rendering a testimony with which the
most careless observer can hardly fail to be
struck.   To begin with, it testifies that the
period of great crimes and odious vices is that,

not of the earlier, but of the later years.
Solomon's after life, when he gave himself up
to heathen women and their idolatries, belied
the promise of his youth. If Tiberius or
Domitian had died after the first half-dozen
years of their public career, their names would
have gone down to history as those of virtuous
and amiable rulers. It was their latter days
that were stained with cruelty and lust. Precisely the same is true of our own Henry VIII.
Had he died at thirty his memory would have
been cherished as that of perhaps the most
popular of English monarchs. In this subject,
as everywhere, Shakespeare shows his unerring
insight. His criminals, his villains, are not to
be found amongst the young. Macbeth and his
wife are no fledglings. Iago, his most detest-
able character, is a man of middle age.

To-day, if any one will carefully examine the
newspapers, he will find that the domestic
tragedies, the business defalcations, the breaches
of trust that cause widespread ruin, are the
work mainly of life's later periods. And what
comes to the surface in newspaper history
represents the merest fraction of what is taking
place daily and hourly in the world around. It
reveals nothing of the breakdowns in men's
faith and hope, of the cynicism that has too
often succeeded to the early enthusiasms, of
the exchange of lofty ideals for lower and

material aims. These things are always hap-
pening, and it is in middle life that they do
happen. George Eliot, one of the surest-eyed
of our modern observers, has again and again
in her works evidenced her recognition of this
fact. In "Adam Bede," Dinah Morris, the
woman preacher, so ethereal and unworldly in
the beginning, settles down later to human love
and marriage, like ordinary mortals. In "Middlemarch," one of the principal characters, the
young doctor, the devotee of science, who,
spurning the vulgar pursuit of gain which
seems to him the disgrace of his profession, has
vowed himself to researches which should
assuage the sufferings of mankind, ends as a
fashionable practitioner, who extorts big fees
from gouty patients.

And if from observations of this kind we
penetrate to the causes of things, and examine
what is really at work in the mind and heart of
man, we realise how natural, one may say inevitable, is all this. We see at once how much
youth has in its favour, from the moral point
of view, as compared with the later time.
Granted that then the passions are hot, and
the desires eager, and that the judgment is not
as yet fully formed nor fortified by experience.
But what advantages there are to counter-
balance this! In the first place, there is the
safeguard youth possesses in the actual pres-

ence and influence of parents and friends of mature age. Whatever these may be in their actual character, they always and instinctively show their best side, and give the best counsels to their young people. For the man of middle-age this wall of defence has been taken away. After forty, there are few people about him whose claims he would recognise to authority over his conduct or character.

But that is not all. While youth is the time of noble enthusiasms, when the recital of great deeds, the history of devoted lives, stir the blood and set the soul on fire, the later period is the time of cooling down, of disillusions, when the spirit droops discouraged, as it perceives life's limitations as compared with the boundless possibilities of its earlier visions. It is the time when the seamy side of things is revealed, when the heroes youth worshipped are discovered to be made, many of them, of very common clay, when hopes deceived and promises broken have brought bitterness to the spirit. It is the time when the mind, having passed in review the different systems of belief which clash and storm at each other in this distracted age, is tempted, with Lucian, to count religion as a deceit and philosophy as a vain thing. It is then men fall into the kind of cynicism expressed once in our hearing by an able man who, when projects of moral

reform were being discussed, exclaimed, " Let
the young fellows try and do something; it is
no use coming to us old ones who believe in
nothing and nobody."

It is the time when, if ever, men become
gourmands and libertines. At a city banquet
a magnate was overhead to say to his neighbour, " At our time of life what is there left
but the pleasures of the table ? " It is the
period when, with no one in authority to
restrain them, with earlier convictions blunted,
possessed of pecuniary resources such as were
denied in earlier years, they are most likely to
yield to sensual gratification. Those who have
paid any attention to the statistics of immo-
rality know what facts could be adduced in
support of this. By whom are houses of
debauch chiefly maintained ? The answer
which comes from the Continent as well as
from our own land is that it is not by the
purses of the young so much as by those better
filled of men of middle-age.

These are also the dangerous years in the
history of domestic relationships. In Tolstoi's
terrible novel, " The Kreutzer Sonata," he
depicts with grim and naked realism the
history of a married couple who are ill-suited
to each other. In the first years of their
wedded life the elements of discord are kept
under, partly from the fact that each one is as

yet under an illusion as to the real character of the other, and partly from the passional attraction which youth and beauty mutually create. But later, when character on both sides has been laid bare to the roots, when youthful ardour has cooled, and when the germs of disagreement have had time to fully develop, a condition of things which before was difficult has become intolerable, and all ends in terrible tragedy. The stern Russian moralist declares that in writing the story he has been delineating the features of innumerable domestic interiors. He would have us believe that, barring the tragedy and the blood, this is almost the normal condition. We would fain hope things are not so bad. But this much may certainly be said : that where a marriage is ill-assorted, and the germs of disunion do exist, it will be precisely in these after years that the position will become most strained, and an open scandal most to be dreaded. With such an ill-starred pair, the forces which hitherto have worked towards keeping down the discord—the passional attraction, the mingling of the ideal in their estimate of each other, and the sense of delicacy and mutual self-respect—will have steadily diminished in their efficacy, while the spirit of antagonism and the reasons for its exercise will have grown in a corresponding ratio.

Is this the language of pessimism ? Say

rather of precaution. Pessimism is impossible for those who believe the world has been redeemed by Christ. None the less is it wise for us to realise the difficulties of the track we follow, and to prepare ourselves for its most slippery places.

Our subject has its lesson for preachers. While they do their duty by young men, let them not forget the need that others have of counsel and warning. Founding their appeals on a closer analysis of nature and life, they will be the more likely to find them strike home.

And let those of us who are advancing towards "the dangerous years," or who are already in the midst of them, understand that there is absolutely no safety for us, apart from a daily application to those sources of strength which our fathers found sufficient for their need, and which we shall in our day, as did they in theirs, prove to be unfailing.

MODERN REALISM.

THE word Realism is just now a good deal in request. It is astonishing the work that is got out of it in literary and artistic coteries. The reckless way, indeed, in which it is bandied about in criticism makes one sometimes doubt whether there is too clear an idea in the general mind as to what it actually stands for; for it really represents a capital distinction. Realism has a definite philosophy and a definite aim, an aim and a philosophy bearing closely upon the highest religious and social interests It is, therefore, eminently worth our while to understand it and to make up our minds upon its pretensions.

It is curious to note, for one thing, how completely the word itself, of late years, has changed its meaning. The student recognises it as the great watchword of middle-age Platonism in its battles with Nominalism. To-day it is the symbol of the party which abjures Plato and all his works, which holds to the visible, the material, the objective, as distinguished from the absolute and the ideal.

It is in France that the school has its principal seat, and in French literature and art that its characteristics are most strikingly manifested. But fashions are contagious in literature as elsewhere, and the new method is showing itself more or less over the whole European field.

The distinction between it and the opposite school will come out best if we compare their procedure in typical works. The Idealist in literature has his hero; or if not that, there is at least behind all his work an absolute ethical standard by which everything and everybody is judged.

Realism, on the contrary, rejects absolute standards of character. Its moral portrait painting is simply a natural history of temperaments and of passions. In Flaubert's great work "Salammbo," which may be taken as a type, there is not, from beginning to end, a single gleam of moral sentiment. The author awards neither praise nor blame. He simply describes. And this method is adopted deliberately and of set purpose. We are told it is the only true one. The Idealists have been leading man along a false track, teaching him to dream with his head in the clouds, instead of to open his eyes upon the fact before him.

M. Zola, whom English readers will, perhaps, have a difficulty in recognising in the garb of a prophet, regards himself and his co-workers as having a serious mission. They are, he says, the literary exponents of Positivism. In his apologetic work, " Le Roman Experimental," he lays down the canons of the new school. " Our quarrel with the Idealists," says he, "is mainly in the fact that we start from observation and experience, while they start from the absolute." We may have a word on this presently. Meanwhile, we may note some of the characteristics of the method which first strikes the student.

It may be safely admitted that, as a school of observation, modern Realism has toiled indefatigably at what it conceives to be its mission. It has made the novel a mass of information on all kinds of out-of-the-way subjects. Obscure nervous diseases are delineated in the manner of a pathological lecture. The miner and the weaver are followed into pit and workroom, and their *métier* described with a minuteness which it requires a technical dictionary to follow. Not a discovery in science, nor an eccentricity of manner, nor a complication of motive, but is pressed into the service. Realism proposes to be a universal instructor, and it certainly has laboured hard to teach the public something.

The next thing that strikes us in the
Realism of to-day is the absence of all reserves.
There are sides of man's life, functions of his
nature, which hitherto have been recognised as
inferior, and over which proper feeling required
that a veil should be drawn. The new school
knows nothing of this reticence. It regards
everything which belongs to animal sensation
as in its sphere to describe; and it shrinks at
no detail. Connected with this is its preference
for characters where the animal elements are
most in evidence.

But these two features, the accumulation of
external detail and the delineation of the life
of sense and of animal appetite, rest upon one
and the same basis, namely, the philosophy of
life, of which modern Realism is the exponent.
The old teaching placed man above nature.
External details were made use of only to throw
into relief the working of the great entity, the
human mind and soul. The new teaching, on
the contrary, regards man as simply a sensitive
part of nature. His mind is a function of the
brain. Instead of being the *raison d'être* of the
world, he is only a detail of it. Being thus
confounded with universal matter, the Realist
describes him as such. He and the objects by
which he is surrounded are part of the totality
of things, and worthy of the same attention,
neither more nor less.

One could add much to this description. But
it is time, perhaps, to submit the pretensions
of this school to a little examination. To begin
with, What is the value of the statement that
Realism brings us, as Idealism does not, into
contact with the actual fact of things? It
bases itself, we are told, upon " observation and
experience." But what, after all, are the
Realist's observations? They are simply im-
pressions from without, plus the mould which
his own mind, his previous education, his fixed
ideas, give them. He has no more got rid of
subjectivity than his rival. Neither of them
has given us, or can give us, the outside fact in
its naked simplicity.

And here comes another inquiry. Is it, after
all, the business of art or literature to give us
an exact reproduction of Nature? For if so,
we might well ask, Why art at all? Why any
paintings or any literature? What our own
eyes present to us will be surely nearer the fact
than anything on canvas or in print. Or, if we
must have something, then a waxwork figure,
flesh-tinted, will give us a nearer approxima-
tion than a statue of Phidias, a photograph
will be more valuable than one of Raphael's
Madonnas.

Here, then, are two grounds of quarrel with
the Realists. The first is, they do not, after
all, give us the reality; and the second, that in

seeking to do so as their one end, they follow a false method. For the mission of art and literature is not fulfilled by what they reproduce so much as by what they create. It is not here as in science. We do not look for subjectivity in a work on trigonometry. But in literature, properly so called, the value, the interest lie precisely in what we taste of the man himself. Is the poet a mere reproducer of Nature? Does he not rather create Nature for us? Is not Yarrow something more to us because we have Wordsworth's sonnets, and are not the Highlands a new region since Scott threw over them his magic wand? And in art, what is it that makes a picture great, if it is not that it is suffused with the artist's own soul, that we see there the aspiration, the struggle, the inner life, which have made him a man apart? Realism would never have given us " The Transfiguration," nor Michael Angelo's " Last Judgment." Could we afford to be without them?

In contradiction to the Realist dogma we are bold to affirm that the mission of art and literature, instead of being fulfilled by the setting forth of what is, consists rather in helping to create what is not. And for this supreme reason : man is not simply the thing he is to-day ; he is a perpetual becoming ; there is going on in his nature a continuous evolution ;

he carries in him the embryo of a being higher than his present self. In that fact is the perpetual justification of Idealism. The highest excellence may perhaps exist as yet only in the poet's dream; but let him not, for all that, cease to give us his dream; for as we study it, we are on the road to realise it. The poetry of to-day will become the prose fact of to-morrow.

A FRENCH PRIEST.

CHRISTIANITY loses much in every way by the great chasms in doctrine and church order which yawn between its different communions. The worst of it is that we know so little of each other. Saintly lives, careers full of the loftiest inspiration, are to be found in all the churches, if we could only cross these crevasses in search of them. But that is what most of us are unable to do. Who, for instance, of our English Protestant readers have ever heard of the French Catholic priest, Jean Baptiste Vianney? Yet we venture to say that in this century, in which science meets us every day with a new marvel, there has been nothing more astonishing than this man's life and ministry. It is thirty years since he died, but his biography, a bulky volume by the Abbé Monnin, is still running through edition after edition in the Catholic world, and the subject of it, being dead, yet speaketh.

Our clerical readers who are considering whether there are any new features which they

may profitably introduce into their work, would
do well to study the type of ministry here presented. It is a type entirely different from
their own, one surrounded by beliefs and
methods with which they will have little sympathy, but which, nevertheless, has in it features
which no earnest man can study without much
pondering, and some searching of heart.

M. Vianney was ordained in 1815, and soon
after was appointed Curé of Ars, the village
which, by his unparalleled labours, became,
before his career was over, a centre of Catholicism in one sense more real than the Vatican
itself. He entered it when it presented few
features calculated to inspire or encourage.
It was a little out-of-the-way parish near
Lyons, whose people were religiously indifferent, weighed down with poverty, and possessed
of the fierce, hard greed characteristic of the
French peasant. Virtue was at a discount.
On Sundays the people assembled on the green
or in the cabarets for dances and diversions of
all kinds, with results disastrous to morality.
The young curé set to work. His ministry was
of the pulpit, of the street, of the fireside, and
of the sick chamber. Step by step he led the
people along the path of reform until the
parish, to judge from the description given of
it, resembled nothing so much as Kidderminster
in the days of Richard Baxter. Peace and

prosperity reigned in the place. It became an abode of faith and love.

The church, which on his arrival was in a ruinous condition, was enlarged, renovated, and beautified. Here are some of his ideas about the place which the House of God and its services should occupy amongst a population. They are worthy the attention of Protestants. " Man," says he, " must have his holidays, his *fêtes*. The Church knows it, and provides them, and it is the only institution which provides such as gladden him and, at the same time, elevate him; they cost the people nothing; the church is open to all; lights gleam in its noble interior; thrilling music thrills its vaults, and penetrates the heart. All the splendours reserved for princes in their palaces are here offered the people as their own in the house which is theirs and God's; in the church, and there only, the humble are treated as the nobly born offspring of God."

These were his thoughts for his people. What were his thoughts for himself? We are in a region strange to modern Protestantism when we speak of his ascetic discipline. It is an instructive chapter if only as a study in psychology. Let us grant that he carried his ideas to an extreme. There seems not the slighest danger that people will rush too quickly to an imitation of them. His domestic affairs were looked after by a pious widow, who, however, did not live in the house. She had to watch for opportunities of getting in and putting things in order. There were struggles on this point between her and the curé, which would be amusing if they were not so pathetic. The good soul was bent on securing him some comfort, which he was equally determined not to allow himself. What was her despair at finding one article after another of his furniture disappearing in gifts to the poor, till there was almost nothing left! Well-cooked dishes were sent in to him, but mendicants feasted on them and not he. A meal with him would consist of a couple of potatoes, or of a few mouldy crusts. "I am happy," said he, "to eat the bread of the poor. They are the friends of Jesus Christ. It seems to me, when I do so I am at the table of our Lord."

It is time we gave some inkling of the labours our curé got through on a diet like this. We have spoken of the transformation effected in his parish. But his work there represented only a very small fraction of his actual ministry. What will our readers say to a pastorate to strangers flocking to him for spiritual help, whose numbers during a long course of years amounted to an average of some eighty thousand per annum?

The origin of these pilgrimages, for anything

parallel to which we have to go back to the times of Peter the Hermit, or of Francis of Assisi, was quite simple and natural. At first it was the elect souls, those who thirsted after God and yearned for a higher life, who were drawn to a man who seemed to breathe a diviner air, and to know the secret of the spiritual world. The poor also began to flock to the philanthropist who, having nothing, seemed yet to be ever giving. Later on tidings of miraculous cures brought to the parish crowds of persons afflcted with every species of bodily ailment. Then the sorrowful, the stricken, those who had lost heart and hope, began to discover that Ars contained a man with a heart of gold, with a sympathy all-embracing, and with a measureless faculty of consolation.

But even these crowds did not represent the measure of his influence or of his toil. Every morning his table was covered with a pile of letters, all repeating, with infinite variety of detail, the same story of doubts, difficulties, sorrows, sins; and entreating his advice and his prayers. Mothers wrote about erring sons, wives about faithless husbands, bishops and heads of great religious societies sought his aid on questions connected with their charge. Men distinguished in letters, or occupying brilliant positions in society, sick of the world, but unable to believe in religion, asked for his secret of faith. This priest was indeed drinking of the cup his Master drank of. He seemed to be bearing, with Him, the sorrows of humanity.

Let us give a sketch of his average workday. It is surely unparalleled in the annals of any ministry. From the time he entered his humble abode in the evening, which was at nine in the summer and seven in the winter, the crowd of strangers of all classes and conditions, anxious for an interview, began to gather in the vestibule of the church facing the parsonage. Each one kept his place during the night, until the opening of the doors, which took place ordinarily at one or two in the morning. This was the hour at which the curé commenced his task. The work of interviewing went on without interruption till seven, when he said the morning Office. After this he entered his house and took a little milk by way of breakfast. He then continued until ten, when, shutting himself up in his sacristy, he gave himself to private prayer. On coming out he had a reception for the infirm, and for those who were unable to prolong their stay at Ars. Ordinarily the crush at this time was immense, such that the curé was in danger of being carried bodily away. At eleven o'clock he preached. On coming down from the pulpit he was more surrounded than ever. People forced letters into his hands, money for charitable objects, relics that he might bless them. Mothers presented their children for benediction, the infirm on their knees before him barred his passage. The hour of his midday meal was the time when he ran through his immense correspondence. Afterwards he paid his daily visit to his orphanage—an institution conducted on similar lines to that of Mr. Müller—again having to pass through a crowd of suppliants. He then said vespers, and continued the work of confessing till five o'clock. His day finished by a series of brief interviews to people who were not able to remain longer. Between seven and nine he retired for his few hours of silence and repose. It seems incredible, but his biography declares that this routine was continued *without a holiday* for well nigh forty years !

We have hinted at supposed miraculous cures. The subject of faith-healing is a large one, which it is impossible to discuss here. At Ars, however, it is certain that during the long years of M. Vianney's ministry cases were constantly occurring in which either the deaf heard, the blind saw, and the lame walked; or else a vast number of people were deceived into believing as much. If every one of them were proved false, there would, however, remain this one miracle, that of the man himself, exercising during these decades of years his prodigious ministry, existing, one might say, almost without food, rest, or sleep—a man who, though followed by an amount of homage reaching almost to adoration, never swerved from the line of humility and self-abnegation to which he had committed himself.

A word may be said as to the homilies which formed part of the curé's daily instruction. They were, in his later years, entirely unstudied, his sole and sufficient preparation being the constant occupation of his soul with God. His eye would range over the crowded ranks of his auditory, frequently fixing itself on some one, as though he were reading into his soul, and was about to take its secrets for the text of his discourse. The absence of self-consciousness was absolute. People did not think of criticising him. His words made them criticise themselves. Men, saturated with the sceptical spirit of the nineteenth century, as they listened, found themselves transported into another region. He spoke of Christ, of heaven, of the spiritual world, and the Christian life, as one to whom they were the sole realities.

M. Vianney died at his post. After an exhausting day, during the heat of the July of 1859, he tottered into his room, saying, " I can do no more." The eager crowd at the doors next morning were disappointed in their expectation of seeing him. Two days afterwards, in his seventy-fourth year, the faithful servant of God had yielded up his soul.

Why have we written of this man? Certainly not because he was Romanist, but because he was Christian. Surely there is a lesson here, and an encouragement for the ministry of every Church. Who shall say, with a career like this before them, wrought out in the midst of the brilliant and mocking France of the nineteenth century, that a Christian ministry, whatever outer form it may take, provided there be given to it the full devotion of a life, can ever be other than one of the supreme forces of the world? And there is a message from the story wider even than this. It is that the eternal laws of the spiritual kingdom work themselves out apart from our artificial distinctions. Not that principles are to be lightly esteemed. Only we are to remember that the first principle is to love our God with all our heart and our neighbour as ourselves.

ON METHOD IN BRAIN WORK.

THE tendency of modern civilisation is to throw ever more work on the brain. The army of public servants who live by toil which is mainly mental is an exceeding great army, and is constantly on the increase. In the category come journalists, literary men, ministers of all denominations, and a multitude of others less distinctly classed.

The brain worker has his privileges, but, on the other hand, he is in certain respects at a great disadvantage as compared with other members of the community. The peculiarity of his position is that as a toiler he stands alone. The merchant and the tradesman can, for the furtherance of their enterprises, employ an indefinitely large number of helpers. The manufacturer increases his income-earning capacity by adding to the number of his machines. He may be ill, or be taking holiday, but they go on weaving his cotton or forging his iron. And if they get injured, or become old and worn out, they can be replaced by new and improved ones. The literary man or the preacher, on the contrary, carries his whole stock of machinery under his hat. He cannot add to it. Its outfit is subject to rigid limitations. The machine itself is eminently delicate and susceptible to injury. When it grows old, or when by illness or accident its work is interrupted, it cannot be replaced. The worker's earning capacity is brought to a temporary or to a final end.

If, then, we consider the brain simply as a wage-earning instrument, without taking note of the higher aspects of the question, we see here the immense importance for the worker, of a knowledge of the best methods of managing it. What is vital for him to know is, how to get the best from it, both in quantity and quality, without impairing its force.

In what follows it will be, not so much to old hands, as to those who have this experience to gain, that we address ourselves. Seasoned brain workers get to know the conditions, and also the vagaries of their own particular instrument, as no one else can. There are also, it is to be remembered, amongst successful toilers in this line, enormous differences of mental constitution, which make the task of framing a general prescription which shall fit all individual cases a difficult if not an impossible one.

But some principles may nevertheless be

laid down, which are of universal application, and which, while of the first importance
to the beginner, are such as the most experienced
veteran may do well at times to remind
himself of.

The main point to remember is that mental
work is a species of agriculture, and that here,
as in actual farming, the secret of success lies
in a good system of rotation of crops. The
farmer knows that if he goes on raising barley
from the same field for successive years, the
crop will constantly degenerate, and the soil be
impoverished. By varying the crop a fresh set
of elements in the soil is drawn upon, and so
the process of exhaustion is retarded. But
rotation of itself is not enough. The elements
that have been taken out of the land will have
to be replaced. And in addition, the ground at
times will require a period of rest. It must lie
fallow.

Precisely the same obtains in mental production. Every student, for instance, knows the
relief obtained by varying his task. Wearied
with mathematical problems, the mind will
feel a renewal of vigour in turning, say, to the
study of history. But there is another thing
which is not so clearly seen. In each day
the moment comes, with some earlier, with
some later, when the brain can no longer, with
any advantage, continue to absorb facts and

ideas. To toil on then, as so many do, in the same line of effort, is a grave blunder. What the mind picks up in its weariness from such toil it will not retain. And serious risks to its own soundness are being run. But the rest it is now calling for need not be inaction. What is wanted is simply to totally reverse the mental process. Instead of continuing to receive and to absorb, let the student, throwing his books aside, set in motion his *creative* faculties. It will be a positive and delicious rest now to let the mind dream its way along some line of its own, to sketch a character, to project an article, to lay the foundations of a sermon. The experience here is as when one takes a relay of fresh horses on a long journey. It is only one side of the brain that is tired. Another set of faculties, those of imagination, of suggestion, of invention, have been all the time resting, and are now, at our bidding, ready to spring forward, like high mettled coursers, eager for the race.

But on this, the creative side of the mind, again, there are departments and sub-divisions of faculty, the laws of which the trained observer comes to recognise and to make the most of. In the department of suggestion, for instance, there are times when the brain is specially fertile, teeming with crude conceptions, which it does not, however, seem disposed to follow out. The experienced worker will not force the mind here. He will jot down in his note-book these germs of ideas, in all their crudity, and leave them there. They are, he knows, all grist for his mill, and will be ground into fine flour by-and-by.

In connection with these bare suggestions, again, an important law is to be noted, that which physiologists term "unconscious cerebration." It is a familiar experience to writers to find a subject which, at their first dealing with it, refuses obstinately to open up. But, knowing the mind's ways, they are not thereby discouraged. Instead, they leave the topic, as it were, in soak, and coming to it afterwards, without having made any direct conscious effort towards its manipulation, they find that by simply letting it lie in the mind it has softened and become malleable, and that they can now deal with it entirely at their ease. The brain, in such instances, seems to have been working, as the heart works, involuntarily and unconsciously, but not the less effectively.

But the brain-worker, however much he may economise force by methods such as these, cannot for ever remain at his desk. His nature will, in the end, call out for movement, for exercise, for the open air, and it will be at his peril if he disregard the call. But here, also, while giving himself entirely to the business of

5

recuperating, and enjoying the process to the full, as he takes his row on the river, or strides across the moorland, or saunters down the crowded street, he will not lose his time. Another part of his nature will now be brought into play, a part which performs one of the most important functions connected with his daily task. We speak of his faculty of observation. He carries with him the open eye which gathers material from every glance. What this means to the preacher or to the literary artist any one may understand who takes the trouble to analyse a good modern sermon or a first-rate work of fiction. The essence of both will be found to be in accurate observation of men and things. The preacher holds his hearers and the writer his readers by making them see what he has seen, as he has looked into the face of nature, or at the ways of his fellow men. Countless thousands, before Dickens's day, had traversed London, South of the Thames, to find there only the common place and the dingy. But the author of "Pickwick," as he strolled through the Borough, and cast his eye down Lant Street, saw there pictures which, transferred to the pages of his immortal work, have made these quarters for ever memorable. Sam Weller and Mr. Bob Sawyer have here, we feel, the framework which exactly fits them. The artist saw for us, and we live for ever after in the light of his vision. These were studies in the city. It is the same when we come to the country. With what delight does a lover of nature and of human nature read such a bit of description as the walk to church of Mr. and Mrs. Poyser in "Adam Bede"! Was there ever anything more perfect as a study of men and things as they exist in our English Midlands? We have here the work of an artist whose country walks and talks were, in the first place, relaxations from indoor toil, but, in the second place, golden opportunities for obtaining living pictures of nature and of man.

The subject might be indefinitely prolonged, but we have said enough, perhaps, for our purpose, which was to show, as the result of experience, what can be done by care and method in the way of economising that most precious of all motor forces—our brain power.

The human mind is a tree of life, growing by the side of the river of God and bearing all manner of fruits. To guard it sedulously, to study the laws impressed on it by its Creator, to enrich the soil around it, and so to develop it to its fullest stature, and to the limits of its producing capacity, are not only plain duties which a share of our own interest should dictate, but the most fitting acknowledgment we can make to Him who has thus so richly endowed us.

ON RETIRING FROM BUSINESS.

THERE is, perhaps, no idea which the average middle-class Briton finds it more pleasant to caress than that of rewarding himself, a certain number of years hence, for the daily grind he is now undergoing at the treadmill of affairs, by a pleasant villa outside his native town, where he will be able to wake up morning after morning with the consciousness of an adequate balance at his bankers, and at the same time with no business worries to disturb his repose. How often has he gone over the calculation, as to the time that will be required at the rate his business is now developing, before this consummation is reached! The risky speculations in which he occasionally hazards, and at times engulphs, his spare capital is due to his anxiety to abridge this period.

We are not going to say that the step he proposes to take in the dreamed-of future is a false one, but it may very easily be so. To retire from business is, in many cases, to retire from one's manhood, to retire from the exercise of the qualities which make an individual of any value either to society or to himself.

To consider this question as being one simply of pounds sterling is an evidence of a want of realistic foresight, so gross that it is difficult to understand how it can exist amongst men of ability enough to push their way in the world. That it does exist, however, is shown by the number of retirements that are effected on this sole basis. And men do not seem to be deterred by the lamentable results which so often follow.

A moment's consideration of what is involved will show to any moderately observant person that to take a step of this kind is to put much of what is best in a man's life at risk. A man's business has been a large factor in the making of his character. In the earlier and struggling days it was the daily necessities of the position that developed his ready wit, his patience, his power of enduring long strains of labour. And later, when things were on a larger scale, it was the business that gave him the faculty of insight, of quick and sure decision, that taught him how to manage men. It gave him authority and responsibility, and made him the centre of a little world, which in its turn contributed its quota of influence and activity to the larger one outside.

There are men who, at a stroke, will cut themselves off from all this, and step into absolute nothingness, under the idea that, at last, they are going to enjoy themselves! From being persons of influence they drivel into melancholy loungers, carrying wearily day by day the heavy burden of their discontent.

They have retired with the idea of being masters of their own time. They find now that instead time is their master, and that they are serving under a tyrant. It is an appalling position for a grown man, accustomed to something better, to find himself putting on his clothes of a morning, with not the slightest idea of what he is going to do with his day, knowing only that his doings will be of interest or utility to no single human being. He may as well go to bed again. He could reply with Goldsmith, if questioned on the subject, that he finds nothing in life which makes it worth while to get up.

Failures of this kind happen because men have not grasped the principle which can alone make such a step a safe one. The principle is that our life should be in all its parts a continual progress. A retirement from business is wise, and then only, when it can be proved to be a stage in that progress. To give up an active employment is a death. The point to be sure about is that the death will be followed by a resurrection to a yet higher form of life. This is entirely possible, and is often happily realised. It is so in cases where a man has powers and aptitudes for which his business life has furnished no proper outlet. _To give up the old occupation is in these instances to set free a part of him, and that the best part, which has been hitherto chafing in inaction. The giving up is, in fact, the actual entering upon the real business of his life. That was the giving up effected by John Woolman, the American Quaker, whose autobiography, with Whittier's introduction, forms so delicious and at the same time so inspiring a bit of reading. Woolman tells us that finding himself in a lucrative and constantly-increasing business, he got rid of the greater portion of it, because, firstly, he felt that riches would harm both himself and his children; and, secondly, because he felt it his duty, as that of every Christian in a world where so much ignorance and misery existed, to devote a large proportion of his time upon this earth to direct personal effort for the good of his fellows, and the promoting of the interests of the heavenly kingdom. An idea this, like many another from the same source, which it were well for our modern religious world to take to its innermost heart and ponder.

What makes the giving up, at a stroke, of an

occupation which has been not simply a means of livelihood, but a school of character, a thing of so much risk, is the fact that nine men out of ten do not know how to usefully occupy themselves, except under certain conditions. They need the pressure of circumstances—a friendly necessity—to keep them at it. Let this be withdrawn, and they sink by their own weight to that condition of listless vacuity out of which open a hundred short cuts to the devil.

A man who does not wish to make a failure of his closing years, needs, before taking the leap, to ask himself this question, Have I some object in life, apart from the money-making which I am now renouncing, capable of possessing my mind and soul, and of filling each day with ennobling interest and occupation?

What complicates the problem is the habit people have of regarding a certain age, and that a long way off from life's natural term, as one in which some of the great possibilities are over. Propose, for instance, to the average British bourgeois, who at fifty is building his villa with the view of retiring to it from the city, that he should now pursue the personal culture which his earlier years denied him. Suggest to him that there are worlds of thought and knowledge which up to the present have been closed to him,

and to enter upon which will double the range
of his consciousness. Ask him, for instance, to
open acquaintance with the great Continental
languages and literatures, and so to discover
what other first-class peoples, outside the
English circle, are saying and thinking, and he
will ask himself to what madman he is talking.
Put himself to school at his age? Begin to learn
languages at fifty? Preposterous. It is not
preposterous at all. Let our bourgeois bring to
this new occupation the methods and qualities
which made of him a prospero us business man;
let him bestow on it the same attention, regu-
larity, and care of detail, and success will be
certain and the rewards great. He will find
himself upon a path which slopes steadily
upward, where at every step of the ascent the
prospect widens beneath his feet, and where his
spirit, as it takes in the invigorating breath
of the upper air, is filled with the intoxicating
sense of a new life.

But if a man is not sure of himself outside
his business, let him by all means keep in it.
He cannot here follow a better example than
that given by a Northern manufacturer, who
having in middle life achieved a competency,
determined to run his mill henceforth not for
his own personal gain, but in the interests, as
he conceived them, of the kingdom of God. In
the present stage of Christian enlightenment

there ought to be hundreds of such mills and mill-owners at work in England to-day.

The thing to beware of in this matter is, we repeat, the retiring in any sense from the fullest exercise of our mental and moral faculties. The examples of a Gladstone, a Beaconsfield, a Bismarck, a Moltke, as well as of multitudes of men of lesser note in all departments of affairs, show how, with proper care, a long career full of overflowing life may be continued up to the very end. There can be no better thing for a man than that death, when it comes, shall find him in his working dress, toiling with all his faculties for the progress of the world.

YOUNG ENGLAND AND CULTURE.

THE conflict of races is entering on a new phase. Europe is still an armed camp, but it is evident that the forces which make against war are constantly increasing, and are causing the resort to arms to become more and more difficult. The struggle for national supremacy is as keen as ever, but it is on a different arena, and with other weapons than of old. The question now is, as to who shall lead the world in commerce and science, in art and moral force; and that, again, resolves itself into this other, as to what nation is at this moment producing the best specimens of human nature, in the points of body, of brain, and of inner character.

It is a battle of culture. In what follows I propose, as the result of an experience which has brought me into contact with both young England and the young Continental of various nationalities, to try and point out how in these matters the account stands between them.

We begin with physique. That comes naturally first, for it is the basis of all else that is in a man. Herbert Spencer has put it with an almost rude emphasis when he says that the first condition of success in life is to be a good animal. If a man is to go far, he will need not only to have a good head on his shoulders, but a stomach underneath that understands its duties. The secret of the intellectual supremacy of Greece lay not simply in the training of the porch and the academy, but in its Olympic games.

When we ask how the English youth compares in this respect with the foreigner, the answer is, on the whole, distinctly in his favour. The Duke of Wellington said the battle of Waterloo was won in the playing-fields of Eton. The English lad still believes in his playing-fields, and it is well that it is so. His instinctive love of the open air and of hardy sports is a strong point. It counts for him in the international race that, while the young Frenchman or German spends his leisure in the *café*, over dice and billiards, or worse, he prefers to seek the open on his bicycle or to stretch his limbs in the cricket-field.

It is interesting to observe how generally our superiority in this respect is conceded on the Continent. Last summer, while making an Alpine ascent, I asked the guide who in his opinion were the best climbers. Without hesitation he replied, " Your countrymen, monsieur. They have no equals for courage and endurance." The response coincided curiously with the remark I had met with the day before in a Swiss novel. A traveller had just accomplished a difficult ascent. His guide observes, " You are English, monsieur ? " " No." " No ! I am astonished. I thought that none but English could have climbed at that pace ! "

This is a reputation we shall surely do well to maintain. There are dangers in modern England which gravely menace it. The chief of them undoubtedly is the overgrowth of our great cities. Plato knew what he was about when, in his " Republic," he ordained that when a community had reached the limit of 4,000 families, the overplus should swarm off and found a new settlement. If we do not kill London, London, with its fogs and its de-oxygenated air, will kill us. Nothing is clearer than that unless we mean to dwindle into a bloodless and muscleless race, we shall have to find some means of depopulating our monstrous cities and of repeopling the deserted country.

But in man the physical exists, we may say, for the intellectual, as that, in its turn, exists for something still higher. Let us now, on

this intellectual side of culture, draw attention
to our English young manhood, as compared
with its foreign competitors. It would be
pleasant to be able to record, in a department
so important, the same verdict as in that just
noticed. But we fear the facts are against
us. Take, for instance, our standing with
reference to modern languages. France, it is
true, is not in this respect a strong competitor,
for the French notoriously are indifferent
linguists. But where are we? A short time
ago, at a popular Continental resort, I over-
heard a gentleman, whom I took to be English,
speaking very good French. I complimented
him on the fact, remarking that it was so rare
to hear good French spoken by an Englishman.
"Pardon me," he replied, "I am not English,
I am American. It is well known," he added,
laughing, "that your countrymen are the
worst linguists in the world." I was fain to
acknowledge there was truth in the allegation.
Compare our young men in this respect with
those of Germany, of Holland, of Switzerland,
or Greece. In any of these countries it is the
exception rather than the rule for the young
members of respectable families to speak less
than two languages besides their mother
tongue, while frequently they will have a knowledge of three or four. How many of ours can
speak one? And yet both in commerce and in

the polite world proficiency in this matter is now admitted everywhere to be of the first importance.

There are other departments of study in which our average English youth would hardly, we fear, fare better in the contest. What, for instance, does he know of mathematics ? When Miss Fawcett achieved her triumph at Cambridge a story was told of a professor who, not long before, had declared his conviction that there was not a woman in England who understood the principle on which the rule of three was based. The ladies have certainly had their revenge for that sarcasm. It would be curious to know, however, what proportion of our young men in business who have left school for two or three years could stand an examination on this one point.

It would be easy to add to this indictment, and to point out in a score of other directions the mental nakedness of the land. Be it understood I am not here speaking of those who go to our universities, but of the sons of the middle classes who have received the ordinary commercial education. It is a fact that their Continental competitors of the same rank are working much harder and going much further than they in the intellectual preparation for life. The training of our middle-class schools has been weak in the points where it ought to have been strong. It is improving, but there is enormous leeway to make up. Meanwhile, if in these pages I have the ear of any young men whose schooling is over, let me counsel them at all costs to continue their education. Let them be satisfied with nothing less than a speaking knowledge of at least one of the great European languages, and a working acquaintance with some branches of mathematics, the science *par excellence* of pure reasoning. It is fatally easy to get a glib newspaper acquaintance with things. But the young Englishman must have something more than that if in the present day he is to hold his own.

There remains one other department of culture to be considered, and it is the highest of all—that of the inner character. After all, the physical and mental powers are but the agents and underlings of the really central part of us. These last, indeed, may be compared to the mercenary troops of the Middle Ages. They will fight on either side. A knowledge of languages may be used to disseminate moral poison. A familiarity with the principles of mechanics may be utilised to fabricate infernal machines. The moral part of culture is, then, evidently its vital part. And the nation which on this side of its training possesses at once the best system and the most solid material on which to work will, we believe, whatever its other drawbacks, come out first in the end.

Taking once more our comparative view, we ask, how stands Young England as related to other lands in its culture of the inner life? We here call to mind the remark of an eminent French critic who laments the disadvantages under which his young countrymen labour in this respect as compared with the English, in that while the former universally reject the religion they have been taught in childhood, and are thus cast on the world without a faith, the latter are brought up in a religious and moral system in which they continue to believe.

There is truth in this, and it means a gain on our side which it is impossible to overestimate, for its faith in Christianity has saved England before, and will save it again. Therein has it found the true system of moral culture. The method of Christianity is simple. It is that of completing our nature by its union with a higher. As the bodily nature exists for the intellectual, and the intellectual is the basis of the moral, so the moral seeks its completeness in that Divine nature which overshadows it, and of which it is the imperfect reflection.

There is no more urgent business for England to-day than to see to it that its young people of every class get a training for body, mind, and inner life which shall develop their nature to its fullest strength and on all its sides. There is no other way of keeping the place won for us by our fathers in the van of the world's progress.

HOW PREACHERS ARE MADE.

A HOMILY FOR THE FREE CHURCHES.

THOSE who would forecast the future of the Free Churches need, for one thing, to take account of what is passing in the common rooms of their colleges. There are to be found our preachers in the making. The ideals they are setting up will determine to a large extent the kind of leaders the Church is to have in the coming generation. What are those ideals? Any one acquainted with the inner life of the colleges finds himself in contact with two contrasted theories, which now, as in former days, divide student opinion. The one is, that the time spent at college should be, above all other things, devoted to the acquirement of exact and varied scholarship. The other, that the study of books and of sciences is secondary to the acquirement of the art of effective preaching. The latter idea will, it is safe to say, have its advocates in every class of theological students. Their way of expressing it is somewhat as follows :—" We are not here to be turned into spectacled pedants. What is the use of stuffing ourselves with the forgotten metaphysics of dead and buried ages ? The Churches don't want Dryasdusts. They need live men who know how to put the Gospel into Queen's English. They want speakers. Effective oratory is a great and difficult art, and what we are here for mainly is to learn it." This theory determines a certain line of conduct in him who holds it. Greek and Latin are skipped. Mathematics are treated as of small importance. Instead, our budding orator reads the sermons of popular preachers. He fills his evenings, as far as college regulations will allow, with engagements at tea meetings, Temperance societies, and debating clubs, where he neglects no opportunity of making his voice heard. By this means he gains a fluency which he regards as a veritable gift of oratory, and a guarantee of his success in the future.

The theory and method thus sketched are specially agreeable to a class of young men in our colleges, in many ways estimable, and who are worth winning to a truer ideal. They have become students for the ministry fresh from the excitement and emotion of some great religious movement in which their spiritual life has been commenced and developed. With a soul all aflame they have turned aside from

secular pursuits to devote themselves entirely
to the service of the Church. They have been
hitherto conspicuous in prayer meetings, in
Sunday-school work, in cottage services, and
have found their delight in pouring out there
the fresh experiences of their new life. But
they enter college to find themselves confronted
with tasks to which they are unfamiliar, and
which appear to have no relation at all to the
spiritual life. What is there in Latin declen-
sions and in Greek particles to kindle their
fervour? What spiritual nutriment is to be
found in a proposition of Euclid?

Their first feeling under these circumstances
is one of despair. Later, they compromise
matters. The "secular" studies are gone
through as a necessary evil, while all the time
that can be won, and all the energy of the soul,
are put into pursuits which to them are so much
more congenial. We have said these young
men are worth winning to a truer ideal. It
will not be difficult, we think, to show that
their present one is wholly false. We may
look at it first from an historical point of view.
One of the advantages of living in this late age
of the world lies in the great space of time and
the vast range of facts which it offers us on
which to base our inductions. Regarding, then,
the question of preachers and preaching from
this standpoint, we ask what kind of men have

they been who in ancient or modern times have
made their mark as potent spiritual forces?
What has been their training? Have they
been such as have thought lightly of that severe
drill of the intellect which our best college
curriculums impose? Were they men who
thought religious emotion, spiritual excitement
and ecstacy, sufficient as a preparation for their
work? As our mind travels back to the past
in quest of an answer a multitude of pictures
present themselves. One stands out with
special vividness. It is that of Ignatius Loyola,
the founder of the Society of Jesus, sitting as a
humble learner on the rude benches of a school
at Barcelona, and tugging there at the rudi-
ments of the Latin grammar. He who was to
be the chief of one of the most powerful
religious organisations the world has ever seen,
up to his conversion one of the gayest of
courtiers and most gallant of warriors, now,
with a determination to impress upon his fellow-
men the religious convictions which had changed
his life, realised his ignorance and felt that
at all costs it must be overcome. He tells us
what a trial this was to him, how the tearing
himself away from his spiritual rhapsodies for
the dull round of the scholar's toil was like
exchanging Paradise for purgatory. But he
kept to his task, following up the school with
the university, because, with the rare sagacity

which characterised all his career, he understood that in order to make any permanent mark
upon the world his religious fervour must have
behind it a disciplined and well-fed brain.
And what he enjoined on himself he made a
condition for his associates and followers.
This society became, in his lifetime, one of the
ruling forces of Europe, because his fellow-
workers, Lainez, Xavier, Bobadilla, and the
rest, joined to a passionate spiritual fervour
the most complete intellectual drill.

We have fallen here on an example in the
sixteenth century. Whether we go backwards
or forwards from that date in quest of facts
the result is the same. If we mount the stream
till we reach the early ages of the Church, we
find the great Christian leaders there, the
Augustines, the Basils, the Origens, were men
filled with all the learning of their time. They
commanded the respect of their own and after
ages, not simply because they spoke with
fervour, but because they *had something to say.*
In this matter also modern history is in strict
accord with ancient.

As we cross again the sixteenth century on
the way back to our own times, and ask how
the mighty Protestant teachers of that age,
how the Luthers, the Calvins, the Zwinglis and
Farels were trained, we discover that it was
not on tea-meeting speeches and debating

society rhetoric. They were students first and speakers afterwards. And they became such mighty speakers because they had been such mighty students. In our own land, a century later, we come upon the grand, unearthly figure of Baxter, the greatest spiritual force of his time. Where could the advocates of celestial fervour, as a qualification for the Christian ministry, find a more shining example of it than here? But was it his fervour only that gave him his power? Baxter led both ministry and laity because he was a saint who was also a scholar. Here was a man who wrote Latin as easily as his mother tongue, who was familiar with every phase of philosophy, and who knew the fathers and the schoolmen as the modern minister knows his newspaper. What Baxter was to the seventeenth Wesley was to the eighteenth century, exerting upon it and the time that was to follow an influence even more intense and far wider in range. His followers for a long time had almost the monopoly of enthusiasm in religion; but their leader—was enthusiasm his one and sufficient qualification? This man, the evangelist of Cornish miners and of Kingswood colliers, the field preacher who wrestled with the brutality of eighteenth century mobs, was also the Oxford don, the elegant and accurate classical scholar, the accomplished linguist who, with a mastery of English which makes his style matchless for nervous force and limpid clearness, could preach also in two or three Continental tongues. But we need not prolong this side of the discussion. Otherwise in the last generation we should have to point to Robert Hall in England and to Chalmers in Scotland, both prophets of their time and to their countrymen, whose severe intellectual discipline points once more the lesson we are teaching. In a time such as ours, so intellectually acute and at the same so profoundly disturbed, in which the reasons for faith are being everywhere probed to the bottom, in which every social institution is called in question, and in which existing church systems are melting down before our eyes to give way to a new and larger order, what kind of figure will men cut whose qualifications as spiritual leaders consist simply of emotional fervour, expressed in tea-meeting rhetoric? Certain it is that, delivered up to such teachers, the Church would cease to be a factor in the coming evolution.

The idea that a severe academical course tends to make a man a Dryasdust is a chimera. If a man has the speaking, preaching faculty in him, the repression of it for a time will be an unmixed good. It will surge up again when wanted, developed and purified, to serve now as an instrument for expressing ideas of genuine value.

Nor is it true that a discipline of this kind militates necessarily against the spirit of earnest piety. The ardent enthusiast whom, in this article, we have specially in mind is apt to confound piety with its excited expression in public meetings. He has not yet learned that an even better exercise for it is in the severe self-repression which keeps him silent for years—a self-repression in which he is closely imitating his Master, the carpenter of Nazareth, who up to His thirtieth year kept Himself hidden from men. Let this hard and secret toil be taken up, as Loyola used to say, "*ad majorem gloriam Dei*," and it will be found to be a means of grace. And if, moreover, he desires a present sphere of direct spiritual influence, let him, as did Wesley at Oxford, seek to lift the college life around him to the level of his highest aspirations; let him help his fellow-students to be more spiritual, more unselfish, more complete in their self-dedication, and in this double process of giving and receiving he will find soul and mind to be expanding together, and his preparation going prosperously forward towards a ministry worthy of the name.

LIFE'S UNKNOWN QUANTITIES.

EMERSON has, in one of his essays, a striking passage in which he speaks of the way in which the machinery of society adapts itself almost automatically to the varying fortunes of the individual. A man in the heat of passion commits some crime which, in his earlier years, would have seemed to him impossible. When he comes to himself it appears incredible that he should have done such a thing. He finds, however, society, with its police, its magistrate, its dock, its criminal procedure, calmly and methodically dealing with this phase of his career as though it had been waiting for it through all his years. It is a somewhat grue-some reflection, but there is an idea underlying it which may be carried further. The varied apparatus of civilisation, and its startling rela-tion to us under certain contingencies, suggests an even more complex structure and its rela-tions—that, namely, of our own organism and inner consciousness. It would be a bewildering calculation to endeavour to total up the sum of

all the phases and shades of thought and feeling
passed through by a fully-developed modern
man in the course of a lifetime. But the calculation would, after all, be simple when compared with another—that of the experiences
which, through that lifetime, have been possible
to such a nature, but into which it has never
entered. There is something eerie in the
thought of the pictures which . our inner
machinery is prepared to throw at any moment
upon the screen of our consciousness, but which
will never come there. The precise sensation
realised by a person when threatened by a
terrible catastrophe, such as death by burning
or by murder; or that, on the other hand, felt
on the news of the coming to us of a great
fortune, is what few among us will ever know.
None the less the registering apparatus for the
production of that sensation is already within
us, and would, on occasion, produce it there
with infallible accuracy. Poets have often
chosen psychological themes as the subject
of their muse. They have written on Hope,
on Memory, on Imagination. There is
clearly a field open for another great poem
—the Unrealised Possibilities of Consciousness.

But the subject of life's unknown quantities
is not exhausted by this class of consideration.
Another side of it emerges when we come to

study, not simply the existing capabilities which
are never called into action, but the possible
further development of the capacities themselves. We are ridiculously ignorant, most of
us, about our own powers. There are stops in
our organ which we have never tried, and
which perhaps contain our finest tones. Sir
William Hamilton's story of the servant-girl
who, in the delirium of fever, repeated the
Psalms of David in Hebrew, from having over-
heard her clerical master daily read them aloud
—a feat quite impossible while in health and in
her ordinary mental condition—shows the latent
capacities of an untrained memory when raised
a little above its normal state. What is true of
the memory is, we may suppose, equally true of
all our powers. Evolution suggests that every
faculty we possess is as yet in a rudimentary
condition. Some of those destined in the future
to play the most important *rôles* in the human
drama are hardly, as yet, above the horizon.
The faculty of second sight, for instance, so
abundantly testified to as existing amongst the
Celtic races ; and the mysterious powers, baffling
completely our Western science, shown by
Eastern yogis, we may well believe are part of
our common heritage, if we knew only where to
find and how to train them. It is curious to
reflect what a revolution might come in our
view of the universe by the development in us

of a new organ of perception. A fresh window
let in to the wall of our consciousness might
make our knowledge of the spiritual world as
certain as that of the planetary system, and
cause Agnosticism, Pessimism, and Materialism
to be tenable only in Bedlam. And no sound
Evolutionist will say that such an organic
development is impossible. The outside universe contains innumerable unknown quantities;
and that man has, in his microcosm, the elements which answer to them all, may be far
more than a poetic conceit. What Goethe said
of the Divine immanence has its meaning also
for man—

> Ihm ziemt's, die Welt im Innern zu bewegen
> Natur in sich, sich in Natur zu hegen.

The unknown about ourselves presents itself
also very vividly when we consider our daily
changing relation to environment. We do not
need to have read Kant to discover that our
consciousness from moment to moment is a
compound of the action of our internal
perceptive organs and of the play upon them
of the external world. How far the variations
in the second of the conditions is capable of
influencing our subjective states is what none of
us is sure about. Glycerine by itself seems the
most innocent of substances, but one of its
combinations forms the most terrific of

explosives. In like manner natures that
for years have seemed to themselves and to
their neighbours born to simplicity and to
quietness have, by combination with new
circumstances or new personalities, developed
into tremendous forces of revolution or of
crime. The devout gentleman - farmer of
Huntingdon never in his earlier years
imagined that he would one day make the
name of Cromwell so feared, hated, and
admired. Had not his uncle, the reigning
Pontiff, insisted on his joining, as a young
man, and against his own will, the Papal Court
at Rome, Alexander VI. would probably have
led a peaceful and unnoted career, instead of
making the name of Borgia the symbol for
everything execrable in cruelty, hypocrisy, and
vice. Of humbler men the same is true. As
Ruskin says : " The virtues of the inhabitants
of many country districts are apparent, not
real ; it is only the monotony of circumstances
and the absence of temptation which prevent
the exhibition of passions not less real because
often dormant." Considerations of this kind
may well bring charity into our judgments of
others, and destroy overweening confidence in
our estimate of ourselves. The result of the
study of the unknown quantities in our own
character, and in the environments to which it
has yet to relate itself, should make us realise,

as each new day begins, our absolute dependence for spiritual upholding and progress on Him whose knowledge is perfect and whose promised aid is adequate to our utmost need.

THE CHURCH'S SONG.

It is a fact worth noting that the number of hymns extant is computed at not less than 400,000, distributed over 200 languages. The stream of Christian song, rising out of the faith and love of the first ages, has, with the growing centuries, widened and deepened, fed from a thousand different sources, until it has now the breadth of an ocean, and a voice as the sound of many waters. It may be perhaps said that in a great hymn, set to noble music, and sung by a multitude whom its thought fully possesses, the soul reaches its highest intensity of religious feeling. It gets above preaching, for preaching is mainly plain prose, while this is beyond either prose or poetry. Prose is thought wedded to appropriate language. Poetry is prose carved and sculptured. Sacred poetry is this sculptured prose relating itself to the most exalted of all possible themes. But Christian song climbs higher than this, for it is sacred poetry caught up on the wings of divine music, and bearing upwards

7

to its own realm the souls whom it has touched
and fired.   In such moments men get a glimpse
of what Handel felt in writing the " Hallelujah
Chorus," when, as he himself described it, " I
did seem to see the heavens opened and the
great God Himself."

And so it comes about that the maker of one
true hymn may live longer in the Church's
memory than the preacher of a thousand
eloquent sermons.   Newman's sermons are in
many volumes on our book-shelves, and are
held in great estimation by those who read
them.   But the masses of Christendom know
Newman and love him chiefly for the one
plaintive strain which, sick in body and
distressed in mind, he threw off when afar
on the blue waters of the Mediterranean.   It
is not the Cardinal, nor the author of Tract 90,
with whom they sympathise, but with the man
who wrote

Lead, kindly light, amid the encircling gloom
Lead thou me on.

The memory of Mr. Binney will long live as
a preacher who, perhaps more than any other
of this generation, represented the English
robust common-sense as applied to religion.
But we are not sure whether the memory of the
writer of " Eternal Light, Eternal Light," may
not survive that of the preacher at the Weigh
House.

One could write volumes on the part which
has been played by hymns in the history of
religion. Their mark is on every age of the
Christian Church. There come to the mind, as
it muses on this subject, " the hymns and
spiritual songs " of which Paul speaks to the
Colossians, and " the praises " which he and
his companion Silas sang together in the
Philippian dungeon ; the " Nunc Dimittis "
and the " Gloria in Excelsis," which, in their
Greek and Latin forms, were sung by the
Church in the earlier ages ; the solemn strains
of the " Dies Iræ," in which mediæval religion
expressed its awe and dread in thought of death
and the Judgment ; and then the mighty burst
of song in which the Church of the Reformation
expressed its new faith and its new life. We
remember how Luther used to say to his friends
in times of depression, " Come, cheer up, and
let us sing together the 46th Psalm." And the
" Ein feste Burg ist unser Gott " into which he
rendered it has been since to uncounted multitudes of other friends, whom he knew not in
the flesh, a great word of cheer.

From Luther to Frederick the Great is a far
cry, in character more than in time, and yet, in
thinking of German hymnody, the two join
themselves in the mind in a pathetic little story
which readers of Carlyle will remember. On
the night preceding one of his decisive battles,

there came thrilling through the air from one
corner of the camp the solemn melody of this
same hymn of Luther's, which some of the
King's old veterans, as pious as they were
brave, were singing together in an extemporised
service of devotion. As he listened, tears
streamed down the face of the warrior monarch
—Voltairean and sceptic as he was—while he
said to one of his generals, "That means
victory on the morrow." And it did. In truth,
hymns have had a great part in battle-fields. On
the night before Hastings the Normans sang
hymns while Harold's Saxons spent the hours in
carousing. In the seventeenth-century fight
of King and Parliament the Roundheads sang
psalms while the Cavaliers trolled love-ditties.
When it came to fighting, the psalm-singers
proved the trustier metal. When John Hamp-
den fell at Chalgrove, Macaulay tells us how the
corpse of their leader was borne by his sorrowing soldiery to its rest to the lofty but mournful
strains of the Ninetieth Psalm. And if Reformation and Puritan times have their
histories all interwoven with sacred song, so
is it in yet more marked degree with what may
be called the later Evangelical period. The
great revival of the eighteenth century was a
time of new birth to hymnody. Dr. Watts has
been called by Lord Selborne the father of
English hymnology. Doddridge stands out in

this period not only as a sound and excellent divine, but as a sweet singer of Israel. It was in Methodism, however, that religious feeling rose to that height of exaltation, to that intense and fervid glow of faith, needful to the production of song-devotion in its highest form. Methodism may well be pardoned for accounting it a direct providence which placed by the side of Wesley a poet such as his brother Charles, the bard who sang while he preached, who gave the people spiritual songs while he gave them laws. The first glow of that mighty movement has passed away. We need to know what it was in its early intensity to understand the effect of those wonderful hymns. We need to have been at the Foundery, or in the great open-air gatherings at Bristol or in Cornwall, when the multitude, stirred already to its depths by prayer and speech full of solemn and searching truth, gives vent to its feeling in one of these mighty lyrics of the soul. And not in public worship only was the power of these hymns felt. Pitmen sang them as they plied their calling in the depths of the earth; the weavers of Lancashire and Yorkshire softened with their cadence the clash of their looms; housewives and maidens in the busy round of domestic duties kept time to their stirring music.

It requires more idealism than belongs to

the composition of most in this materialistic
generation to entirely understand the feeling
which prompted the Methodist backwoods
preacher to return the title-deeds of a large
farm which had been presented to him by a
friend, after a few months' possession, on the
ground that he was miserable from being
now no longer able to sing this verse of a
hymn, which for years had been one of his
favourites :—

No foot of land do I possess, no cottage in this
  wilderness,
        A poor wayfaring man.
Awhile I dwell in tents below, and gladly wander to
  and fro
        Till I my Canaan gain.

Who can say that man is wholly of this
earth when we have here a brother soul
putting millions of tons of it, reaching from
its surface down to its centre, against one
verse of a Christian hymn, and finding the
ponderous mass, in the scale against these few
words of trust and hope, to kick the beam!
Good hymns, wedded to noble music, may be
potent elements in home training. A family
group on Sunday evening, with mother or sister
at the piano, while the clear treble of childhood
blends with the deeper voice of father and
elder brother in rendering one and another of
the treasures of the Church's song, is a gladsome
spectacle, which becomes in after years a sacred

memory. The strains we hear then weave themselves into the life. Held in the leash of remembrance, they accompany us in the march through the wilderness and give cheer when the spirit faints. " Sing me a bairns' hymn," said Guthrie, as he lay a-dying. The great Christian orator, world-worn and weary, desired nothing better in the closing moments than to have the faith and hope of his life put into accents which fitted his lips when a little child.

It speaks well for a man's career when all through it up to the end he finds his soul stirred, as in the earliest years, by the music of the Church's song and his life keeping time to its holy strain.

INSURANCE AGAINST DULNESS.

THE editor of an American religious newspaper conceived, some time ago, the idea of "drawing" his clerical subscribers on the subject of illustrations in sermons. He sent a circular letter to a number of representative ministers, asking for their views as to the value of illustrations, and of the best method of obtaining and of using them. The topic here suggested is a wide one, and of immediate personal moment to preachers and to churches. Sermon makers and sermon hearers alike believe in illustrations, though many of them would be somewhat puzzled to give a strictly philosophical reason why. There is a general feeling that they light up a discourse. They are, in fact, an insurance against dulness. Young preachers have a fixed belief in their efficacy. We remember an experienced divinity professor who used to excuse the floweriness of many of the deliverances in his homiletical class with the remark that the authors of these poetic effusions would probably be dry enough by the time they reached middle life. He preferred, he said, a little gaudiness to barren sand. A congregation we heard of was apparently of the same opinion, whose secretary, in asking for a second visit from a student in a Free Church college who had favourably impressed them, wrote thus: "We wish to hear again a young gentleman whose name we have forgotten, but who deals largely in stars, flowers, and sunsets." There is an instinct in favour of illustration, especially as a mode of setting forth religious truth. We find it in every language and literature. That fact in itself is an argument in favour of its eventual soundness as a form of spiritual teaching.

But what is illustration? When we examine the matter we find that, whatever form it takes, whether of metaphor, analogy, simile, fable or parable, its essence consists in the setting forth of spiritual truth in terms of matter. It is the using of some lower and more familiar form of experience to explain one that is higher and less known. With the Christian teacher, however, the symbol and the parable drawn from nature are used, not simply as an explanation, but also as an argument. And the argument has, we believe, a strictly logical basis, though it does not seem always to have been clearly apprehended by those who use it. That logical basis may be stated in different ways. One is Professor Huxley's affirmation that matter has two sides—a physical and a spiritual. In this view the sermonic illustration is simply a taking hold of both these two sides and showing their mutual relation. But there is a better statement of the truth than that. It is that the higher forms of life are simply the completion and fulfilment of the lower. The lower and physical is full of prophecy of the higher and spiritual, being linked to it, not simply by likeness, but by essence, the higher containing all the lower in a sublimated form. The business of illustration is to read and accurately interpret the voice of the lower creation as it strains to utter its message about the higher spheres which contain the meaning of its own existence. This sense of the interlocking of all life spheres, of the unity and essential spirituality of the universe, is the finding of our deepest philosophy, and the burden of our noblest poetry. Hegel and Malebranche and Augustine have argued it to the brain; Goethe and Wordsworth and Tennyson have sung it to the heart. Spiritual men in this way always think double. When Thomas Jones, the poet-preacher, as he lay dying, murmured to himself, "My little rill draws near the sea," every word there was two-sided, one pointing matter-wards the other spiritwards. He saw two

things at the same time—the stream dropping
into the ocean, and the soul that had completed
its earthly course letting itself go into the
infinite deep of endless life.

Having got this view of what lies at the
basis of illustration as a valid form of religious
teaching, we are free for one or two practical
comments as to the use of it.   And, first, illustration, to be effective, must take its place as
part of the natural growth of the discourse.   It
is this which condemns the frequent use of
encyclopædias of illustration.   The illustrations
taken there have not grown in the man's own
mind.   They are slop goods, not made to
measure.   However good the material may be,
the article will be a misfit.   A true sermon is
an evolution, which follows very closely that
sketched for us in Genesis.   First, there is
mere chaos, then the glimmering of light, then
the marking of boundary lines.   Later on the
creation becomes green with tree and plant and
populous with life.   The illustrations will come
at the right part of this evolutionary process.
They will leap forth from the treasures of the
man's own observation and of his own reading.
What will give them their special flavour will
be the mixing of his own personality with them.
Richter says a new universe is created every
time a child is born.   That is a strong way of
saying that every man's consciousness is an

instrument which reflects the universe at its own special angle. This personal equation will be found, not only in his first hand observations, but in his reading in science, history, and general literature. The facts which are common to all the world will have their own special message for him, and through him for the people. He will never obtrude his individuality, but the flavour of it in all his thinking will be his greatest charm.

This leads to the observation that perhaps the finest field of illustration is one which a large class of preachers habitually neglect. It is that of human nature as studied from the life. A minister should be a pastor in order that he may be a preacher. A preacher should choose some poor neighbourhood as a hunting ground, not only for souls, but for sermons. A representative journalist once said, "There is copy in every man you meet in Fleet Street, if only you could get him to tell his story." And if there is copy for the press there is certainly matter for the pulpit. Any one who has heard Mr. Moody will recognise that here—in the telling presentation of facts about human life in its multitudinous forms, the humours of it, the pathos, the tragedy, the triumph of it—lies perhaps the greatest element of his power. In coming close to the life of the people, by actual visitation and sympathetic intercourse, a high-minded Christian teacher will confer priceless boons upon a neighbourhood. But we doubt whether what he gives will be more valuable than what he takes away. Such a man can never run dry and never become dry. It is said that Newman sometimes wrote a sermon that it might give him the opportunity of saying one single sentence which he embedded in it. If one sentence can suggest a sermon, a human life carefully studied should suggest many. There are some five millions of these sermon subjects in London alone.

Illustrations serve sometimes to give the hearer a holiday. A great preacher will not hesitate now and then to put his hearers through a bit of hard work, but then, for a reward, he will let them into the playground. They have had five minutes of stiff reasoning. A minute more and they would be looking out of the window. But they will not get that minute. Their leader knows his "psychological moment." At the right point he lets them go. His style has changed. He has flung open the door, and they find themselves in the open field of some quaint personal reminiscence, or of some restful scene in nature where one gets the glint of waters and feels the breezes blowing. How the people enjoy it! They are in the hands of a master who knew that the difficult bit of travelling through

which he has brought them was not only good
to be traversed in itself, but would vastly
enhance the surprise that awaited them at the
other end. The pulpiteer who is not a master
but only a servant, would be afraid of such a
procedure. He is nervously anxious to secure
his little effect at the end of every one of his
oiled and scented sentences, and as a result
produces a sense of dead level and pretty
feebleness.

The pulpit should insure heavily against
dulness. The Church, in the present day,
cannot afford that the phrase "as dull as a
sermon" should circulate as a proverb. Sir
Wilfrid Lawson's prescription against drunken-
ness is, not to drink. In like manner our
recommendation to men whose distinguishing
characteristic as preachers is neither their
orthodoxy nor their heterodoxy, but the fact
that they are hopelessly dull, would be to ensure
against dulness in the pulpit by keeping out of
it.

THE MOTIVE FOR MISSIONS.

THE missionary movement is, like a good
many other things in the Church just now, in
a transition state. The arguments for it have
got to be restated. Many of the considerations
that moved our fathers to zeal in this direction
have lost their power. New horizons have
opened before our generation, and with them a
wholly new class of questions has arisen with
reference to the non-Christian world. If we
examine what is really in men's minds about
missions we find, for one thing, that the modern
science of comparative religion has had upon
them what, for the moment, is a damaging
effect. It is a new revelation to multitudes to
discover that in the Zend-Avesta, in Brahmin-
ism, in the maxims of Confucius, and above all
in Buddhism, there is so much that is excellent.
From this discovery the transition is easy to the
idea that the people among whom these systems
have grown up are well enough off religiously,
without our interference. Let this notion get
firm root in the popular mind, and it will go

ill with missionary enterprise. But it ought not to be difficult to show how utterly unreasonable the idea is. If people will only take the trouble to read their Bibles they will find that all they are arguing for about the worth of outside religions is fully conceded there. The early Christian Church could see inspiration in other systems besides its own. Did it not, to begin with, recognise Judaism, with the whole Old Testament literature, as inspired? And yet Paul and his fellow apostles and evangelists did not find in this anything which made it superfluous for them to carry to the Jewish people the message of Christ! We find, later, such writers as Origen and Clement of Alexandria loud in declaring their belief that the Greek philosophy was, much of it, a revelation of the Divine wisdom. But it seems never to have occurred to them that the mission of the Christian Church to Greek as well as barbarian became thereby annulled. They were too logical to accept the argument that the possession of what was in itself good formed a reason for keeping people out of the enjoyment of what was immeasurably better.

But this is not the only idea that has of late played havoc with the spirit of missionary enthusiasm. Another, very widely spread, is that derived from the supposed unsatisfactory results on

native races of missionary effort. We have all
met the superior person who assures us from
his own observation, or from that of another
superior person he knows, that the native who
has been missionised is infinitely more intolerable than the untouched specimen. This kind
of talk goes round and does its work. What is
the reply? One could easily rush to the mass
of evidence on the other side—such, for instance, as that of Dr. Darwin about the Terra
del Fuegans, or that contained in the changed
condition of South Sea islands, where ship-
wrecked mariners, who would in the old days
have been killed or eaten, are now sure of
hospitality and kindness. But there is no need.
The missionary advocate can afford to be
generous. Let him concede everything with a
grain of truth in it that is said to the dis-
paragement of the evangelised native. Let
him admit that he is often enough a grotesque
specimen of humanity, that his morality is
sometimes grievously at fault, that he can be a
hypocrite, and that he has been known, in
common with professors nearer home, to understand the art of making orthodoxy pay. What,
after all, does this amount to? Simply to what
we knew before, that first steps are apt to be
awkward ones, and that beginnings at improve-
ment often produce effects the reverse of allur-
ing. The log hut and corn patch of the pioneer

settler may easily be condemned as a blot on
the wild beauty of primitive nature. A wiser
criticism recognises in them the commencement
of civilisation. Our unchristianised native may
walk in his old rut with a certain grace, perhaps. But it leads nowhere. To get him out
involves very likely much stumbling and
sprawling. But once out he is free to stretch
himself, and to scale all the heights of progress.
And, moreover, the talk about letting heathen
nations and races alone comes all too late. We
have not let them alone. We are, and have
been, in contact with them at all points, and
the question for serious people is by what
methods, and on what principles, shall that
contact continue to be regulated. We in
England have an enormous responsibility in
this matter. To take India. We have not let
the native alone there. We have, on the contrary, shaken down his government, his political
system, his religious belief. What are we
going to put in their place ? In China we have
not let the native alone. We have burst open
his forts with our cannon, and demoralised him
by millions with our opium. This is a tolerably
heavy account on one side of the balance-sheet,
and it is surely not going beyond the merest
justice to demand that what we have of
philanthropy, of love, and of truth should be
offered these peoples if only in the way of

redress. They have received much of our worst—it is only fair that they should get also of our best.

These are arguments which need to be put boldly before the country, because they rest on solid fact and common-sense, and as such appeal to the wide average of minds. And yet, after all, they do not, and never will, constitute the real motor force of missions, for in the last result it will be found that if Christianity is to spread it is because it is a live thing, and that it is the property of live things to propagate themselves. When the Church ceases to grow it has begun to die. But wherein lies the Church's vitality? Here it is we pass from the practical to the transcendental, to that mystic realm, hidden from the material gaze, where life processes have their beginning. For the Church's life is in the individual contact of its members with Him who is the Life. The men who are the soul of missions, whether in the field abroad or in the heart of the Church at home, are those who have felt within them the mysterious double force of spiritual attraction —its force centripetal and centrifugal. Two voices have spoken to them, one saying "Come" and the other "Go." There has been felt, first, a sense of need and emptiness, drawing the soul to Him who alone can satisfy and enrich it; then, when the heart is filled with a feeling of what life can become, in enjoyment and in possibility of growth, under the touch of Christ, an immense desire comes that men everywhere should share the boon. There is the missionary spirit in its genesis and development.

WOMAN IN EXCELSIS.

(NOT TO BE TAKEN TOO SERIOUSLY.)

SCENE: *After dinner at a "Ministers' Fraternal."*

The assembled brethren are discussing coffee and cigars. Amongst the tobacco clouds are dimly discernible our friends the Rev. CLEMENT OLDWAYS *(host), and the Revs.* HUGH HIGHSPRYTE, ERASMUS BLACKBYLE, WILBERFORCE WITTYER, *and* EUSTACE TWITTERLEY.

TWITTERLEY: I went to hear Mrs. Besant the other night. It was a prodigious draw. The place was crammed. We don't get crowds like that to hear us.

WITTYER: Evidently it takes a woman to make a boom nowadays. If the "Georgia Magnet" were a man, there would not be half the power in his magnetism, I'll wager.

HIGHSPRYTE: Here's to the health of "The Coming Woman." She is going to make us all "sit up," you may depend.

BLACKBYLE: Then may the coming woman be a very long while in coming!

WITTYER: Don't make any mistake, Black-byle. She is already at the doors, and I for one hail her advent. Man has been prome-nading long enough on the page of history, and has, I am bound to say, made himself quite sufficiently ridiculous. It is time the other side had an innings.

BLACKBYLE: With us as spectators and critics! Very well. It will be amusing, at any rate. But I think it is we who will have the fun.

WITTYER: There is more in all this than you think, Blackbyle. We are in a new situation, and woman is the dark horse in it. Man has been in full training for centuries, and we know pretty well where to place him; whereas woman is as yet an undeveloped force.

HIGHSPRYTE: Yes. She is going to upset lots of things. Her first business will probably be to revolutionise the Church.

OLDWAYS: Good heavens! I hope not. What do you mean?

HIGHSPRYTE: Well, don't you see, for one thing, that she is already halfway up the pulpit stairs, and that before you are much older she will be inside the door in full possession?

OLDWAYS: I trust that will not come in my day. I consider it quite unscriptural.

HIGHSPRYTE : It will, unless your day is a very short one. She is there already in America, and fashions of this sort are very catching.

BLACKBYLE : The first thing they will do, I suppose, when they get there, will be to put St. Paul's Epistles into the Apocrypha. The Apostle is too heterodox on their question.

HIGHSPRYTE : Not a bit of it. They will be on excellent terms with St. Paul. They will explain in the sweetest manner that the nineteenth century has outgrown his prescriptions about woman, as it has outgrown those about meats offered to idols.

TWITTERLEY : I don't like the prospect altogether. There are so many things to be considered. For instance, I agree with the saying that "a soft voice is an excellent thing in woman." Now it seems to me if they take to oratory they will ruin their voices. They will get a habit of mouthing and shrieking which will be dreadful.

WITTYER : What nonsense you are talking, Twitterley! Don't you think women know how to manage their voices in public as well as men ? Patti makes more money out of her voice than any man can out of his. I have heard Mrs. Josephine Butler talk to a crowded audience in St. James's Hall. Every word went home, but she didn't either strain or scream.

OLDWAYS : But that is only a small part of the objection. I am convinced that for woman to take a leading part in Church teaching or administration would be disastrous.

WITTYER : Not too loud, Oldways, or Mrs. O. may hear you!

OLDWAYS *(with dignity)* : My wife, sir, knows my sentiments on these points. I am of opinion that woman, lacking as she is in the logical and philosophical faculty, and with her emotional, and I may say, hysterical tendencies, would, if she were in authority, carry the Church into all manner of wild extravagances both of thinking and of practice.

WITTYER : There would be always a sufficiently strong counterbalancing influence.

OLDWAYS : Where?

WITTYER : In the deadly dulness of the average man.

HIGHSPRYTE : That's letting man off too easily, Wittyer. I was going to answer Oldways by asking him a question.

OLDWAYS : What's that?

HIGHSPRYTE : My question is, whether it would be possible for woman in her wildest moods to show us greater absurdities than have been perpetrated by ecclesiastical man?

BLACKBYLE : I don't know what tomfooleries are to be put down to your individual account, Highspryte ; but I am not going to accept your general indictment. Man has a very respectable record in ecclesiastical history.

HIGHSPRYTE : True; and so has woman. But we are talking about absurdities. Could she invent anything more outrageous in the way of doctrine than some of the Gnostic theories, or than the tenets, say, of the Münster Anabaptists ? Could she beat man's record in the way of sect-making ? What do you say of that one which founded itself on the act of contemplating the navel as an aid to devotion, or that of the Taskodrungites, who separated themselves from the rest of the world by the habit of praying with the forefinger on the nose !

TWITTERLEY : You are putting things pretty strong, Highspryte, as usual. What I plead for is the preservation of woman's womanliness. What I am disposed to concede to you is that woman's advent as a teacher in the Church would tend to bring out the tenderer side of spiritual truth, and in that way be a gain.

BLACKBYLE : Stuff and nonsense ! Man thinks woman tender. That is simply his stupid idealism. She isn't tender a bit. In Church history she has been a good deal more savage than man where she has had the chance. It was a woman who demanded John the Baptist's head. The bloodiest religious persecution in English history was under a woman's rule. In France it was Catherine de Medicis who planned the St. Bartholomew massacre.

HIGHSPRYTE: Really, Blackbyle, you ought to consult your doctor. I am afraid he will tell you sad things about your liver; but I am going to tell you how this pulpit contention can be beautifully compromised. Don't look incredulous, Blackbyle.

BLACKBYLE: On the contrary, I am all attention. To watch you riding your very latest hobby will do me more good than any amount of doctoring.

HIGHSPRYTE: I am delighted to think that it is likely to be so useful. But you have made it rather difficult for me to state my idea. What I was going to say was something like this: In the existing condition of things the ministers' wives are regarded as belonging almost as much to the church as to the minister. You have only to carry that a little further. Let colleges be founded for the special education of ministers' wives. Let it be understood that the first qualification for admission is a capacity for public work in the Church. Then, in due time, let each marry a minister and share his pulpit as well as his domicile. Don't laugh, Wittyer. You remember in Plato's Republic marriages are made by the State, and Plato was no fool. In the Moravian Mission Society my plan is how they actually do things. And I understand it works very well.

WITTYER: If I were on that College Committee I should insist that the candidates were at least good-looking.

HIGHSPRYTE: We might allow a large discretion. Madame de Staël was no beauty, but she boasted she could win any man to whom she was allowed to talk for five minutes.

TWITTERLEY: I can't follow you in this, Highspryte. You are cutting at the root of one of my dearest privileges.

HIGHSPRYTE: How so?

TWITTERLEY: My dear fellow, it is in this way. When I am in the pulpit, and my wife in her pew before me, I get a sweet revenge for a week's private lecturing. I hold forth there for a whole half-hour without her being able to open her lips to contradict me. But if she gets the floor in the evening . . . !

At this point in the conversation our informant was, unhappily, obliged to leave. We are left, therefore, to conjecture what, in Twitterley's view, would happen if his wife took the floor in the evening. He adds, however, that to judge by the faces of the other members of the party, a considerable amount of alarm had been created in the minds of the fraternity by the last speaker's view of the new conjugal terrors that might await them in the future.

TYPES OF RELIGIOUS LIFE.

A TRAVELLER, passing through one of our great English manufacturing towns, would find his eye drawn by the varieties of structure of its mills and factories. Some he would see to be massive pieces of masonry, with a certain pretension to architecture, while others would be mere sheds. To the merchant, however, whose interest in the town is in the goods he purchases there, this question of its buildings, whether well or badly situated, whether imposing or otherwise, is one of no importance. The point with him is the quality of the products.

In like manner, as we survey the various structures, of different age and pretension, which crowd the ecclesiastical horizon of to-day, we may take either of these ways of regarding them. We may, for instance, if we choose, pay exclusive attention to their form. Dealing with them thus, we can speak of Anglicanism as an Episcopal form of Protestantism, with its doctrine and discipline contained in the Thirty-nine Articles and in the Book of Common

Prayer; of Methodism as a form of Evangelical Arminianism, with an itinerant ministry; of Congregationalism as a system based on the principle of the autonomy of churches; and so on.

But what, after all, have we learned from this? When we have mastered all the differences in creed and in ecclesiastical order which separate these communions, we are still ignorant of what, if we would really understand their significance, it is most important for us to know, viz., the quality of their products. The kind of inquiry which this age is beginning to get most interested in is, not as to the theoretical peculiarities of this or that system, but as to what kind of men Episcopalians are as distinguished from Methodists, and Congregationalists as compared, say, with Catholics. Do these different bodies produce broadly-marked types of men, and, if so, what judgment may we come to about these types?

As soon as we open an inquiry of this kind we come upon some interesting results. We discover, for instance, that some communions have been much richer in the number and variety of their types than others. And we are taking it for granted here that this richness is in itself a good thing. A dead level of sameness is not admirable anywhere. An age or a spiritual condition which has produced

in abundance boldly-marked individualities
gives evidence of a fruitful soil, and con-
tributes to the enlargement of life on all
its sides. Is not, for instance, the Christian
tradition and ancestry the more valuable to
us in that it contains, not simply the direct
progenitors of the average British Christian
of to-day, but such men as the prophet-
evangelists of the sub-apostolic age, the unworldly figures of a Francis of Assisi, of a
Bernard, of a George Fox, and of a multitude
of others whose habits and life-theories have
been so strangely different from our own?

We have just said that some churches strike
us as much richer than others in their variety
of type. And this, indeed, is what we should
naturally expect. Who could be surprised to
find a system like the Roman Catholic, whose
sway has extended across such vast spaces of
time, and over such immense and diversified
populations, to be much more fertile in this
respect than, say, one of our English Nonconformist sects, with an existence of one or
two centuries, and an influence restricted to
people of the same nationality, and largely of
the same social position?

But when this has been granted it is not
enough to satisfactorily account for what
strikes us, as we survey certain fields of
English religious life, as a curious dearth in

this respect. Take, for instance, our English Congregationalism. It has its one type of minister and its one type of layman. One, and not more than one. Their characteristics are sufficiently familiar. Its minister is a man well - informed rather than learned, married, or if celibate never so from religious principle, progressive in his views both of politics and theology, practical, good-humoured, sincere in his religion and his philanthropy, but without a trace of mysticism, believing in a good dinner, and holding on to this world with both his hands. And the Congregational layman, allowing for differences of position and pursuit, answers accurately to this pattern. He is the English bourgeois *par excellence,* a pushing man of business, respected in his township, prominent in local politics, keenly alive, as well as his wife and daughters, to social advantages, with —just now—a certain vagueness unknown to his fathers in some of his religious ideas, but making up for this by the vividness of his appreciation of mundane things.

Here, again, of mysticism, of idealism, of a world-forgetting devotion to the spiritual side of things, there is no trace. Altogether, the two characters are strong ones, and they form admirable and, we will say, indispensable ingredients of our English life. But they are not enough, and that Congregationalism seems unable to produce other types is distinctly to be quoted against it.

In this respect a much younger body than the Congregational has been far richer. Methodism, in its ministry and laity, offers innumerable reproductions of the type just sketched. But within living memory it has had others of a very different mould. The older generation has vivid recollections of men in its ministry of the Bramwell and Stoner genus ; men who would spend whole nights in prayer, before whose preaching men were stricken down as with shocks of electricity, who, with fast and vigil and hardship voluntarily endured, habitually mortified the flesh, and who, wherever they went, became centres of great spiritual movements, the result of their labours. And the laity of that generation contained such men as William Dawson, the Yorkshire yeoman, who farmed his land for a living, but spent his Sundays and many weekdays in proclaiming, with irresistible and overwhelming eloquence, the principles of that religion by which his whole soul was possessed. And let us not forget that that most daring and original of modern religious movements, the Salvation Army, has had its origin in Methodism. Why could not Congregationalism have produced it ? The question ought to set some of us pondering. A wider question, indeed, may be asked : Why is it that never, by any chance, Congregationalism produces an original —shall we say an extreme type of religious life ? To conceive of a Father Ignatius, or such a man as the Curé of Ars, appearing in its ranks, is beyond the range of the imaginative faculties. There are in the present day men and women born into the world to whom the ascetic life still presents irresistible attractions. Brotherhoods and sisterhoods are springing up to meet the craving of such natures. But these are all outside the Congregational boundary. Within its enclosure one plant grows, and only one. Will it always be so, or will the composite influences of earlier ages, or the study, by some of its younger minds, of other aspects of the inward life than the one to which it at present exclusively holds, avail to break in upon its present monotony ?

Keeping to the present, we may, however, from considerations of the kind just advanced, deduce with tolerable confidence certain conclusions. One is, that a body like the Congregational (to keep to the one instance we have selected for illustration) would never, as it at present exists, suffice for the religious needs and instincts of a whole people. Another is, that the present division of the Church into differing sects serves a purpose entirely separate

from that contemplated by their founders, and
perhaps more useful. They were established
to propagate and defend certain sets of doctrines
and form of Church order. What they have
done is to enrich the world with new individualities.

The Society of Friends has taught the world
some excellent things, but it has put it under
perhaps deeper obligation by producing the
Quaker man and the Quaker woman whom
Charles Lamb has sketched for us so tenderly.

On the whole it is well for us, as we stand
each at our post, doing our best with what we
have of truth to defend and of work to do, to
realise that the Church as a whole is greater
than our part of it, and that outside of our own
struggle and the ends we seek to gain by it,
great laws are operating towards results beyond
our present ken.

CHARLES HADDON SPURGEON.

" There is more love in the hearts of Christian people than they know of themselves. We
mistake our divergencies of judgment for
differences of heart; but they are far from
being the same thing. For my part, I believe
that all spiritual persons are already one." To
these words, which we take from Mr. Spurgeon's last message to his fellows, the sorrowing
sympathy of countless hearts, who now mourn
his loss, has set its seal. For Mr. Spurgeon
was a power, not only over all the English-
speaking world—vast as is the constituency
which that phrase represents—but throughout
the boundaries of Protestantism. His writings,
translated into different languages, have been
spread broadcast in Europe, and to the English
worshipper in the Protestant churches of
France, Switzerland, Holland, or Germany, it
has been quite a familiar experience to hear
quotations from the sermons of their eminent

compatriot in the religious exhortations
there given. At home his presence and work
had become a recognised part of English life,
and Christian people had learned to look on him
as not only a foremost but an almost indispensable religious force. The great career is now
consummated, and we can survey it from end to
end. "Call no man happy till he dies," said
the classic proverb. Mr. Spurgeon is happy in
his death, crowning, as it does, a life lived in
the full blaze of publicity, but against which
no man's finger can point a reproach, and
which, beginning with predictions of failure
from numberless critics, ends amid the universal
esteem of his countrymen and of Christendom.
Middle-aged men send back their thoughts to-
day from the death scene by the Mediterranean
to the beginning of this career, when an
astonished congregation, in an all but deserted
London chapel, woke up to the consciousness
that in the raw country lad before them a new
religious power had appeared, and then on
through the years in which the splendid combination of physical, mental, and spiritual
energy stored there was unfolding itself,
cutting ever broader and deeper channels for
its movement, until by spoken voice, by sermon,
book, and magazine, by religious and philanthropic institution, as well as by the nameless
influence which flowed from so distinct and

original a personality, the Baptist preacher was touching his age at every point. It is all over now; but the generation which has travelled over so large a portion of the life-journey with him in its ranks will not easily forget their fellow-traveller.

In attempting an estimate of his character and work the mind recurs instinctively to that other prominent figure in the religious world who has so recently gone from among us. We refer, of course, to Cardinal Manning. And the association is by no means one entirely of contrast. At opposite ecclesiastical poles in position and opinion, they were alike, not only in being the centre of a vast religious and philanthropic work which bore largely the stamp of their own individuality, but also in some of their mental qualities. They were both marked in a striking degree amongst modern Englishmen by the absoluteness of their convictions. The authority enjoyed by both in the different sections of the Church to which they belonged, and in a large measure outside those limits, was in no small degree owing to the air of finality with which these two entirely sincere men uttered themselves on the subjects of faith. No one could listen to Mr. Spurgeon without feeling that the authority with which he spoke was born of intense conviction. His power lay in realising, as few men do, the things of the spiritual world. To get this in such measure as to make a man in a supreme degree a prophet to his generation seems to demand the working of heredity through many generations. The religious force and insight which made John Wesley the seer of the eighteenth century came to maturity in him, after working through both lines of his ancestors from far back in the family record. The like was true of Mr. Spurgeon. In the family which fled from the Low Countries during Alva's bloody persecution, one of whose members was in Chelmsford gaol in Charles II.'s reign for conscience' sake, and which contained afterwards a goodly line of preachers of the Word, we see the elements slowly forming which were to culminate in this unique religious personality.

We repeat, it was his spiritual force which drew men. Many who did not accept his opinions on more than one outlying religious question, and on some which he regarded as vital, thankfully reckoned him as their teacher because of this. Said Dr. Pusey once: "I love the evangelicals because of their great love for Christ." And multitudes of educated Christian men loved Charles Spurgeon, spite of intellectual differences, for that reason. From the days when Samuel Rutherford so preached his Master as to compel the Duke of Argyll once to cry out, "Oh! man, keep on in that strain," no one, we may safely say, has set forth the claims of Christ to men's love and service with such winning sweetness, with such melting pathos, with such eloquence of the inmost soul as Charles Spurgeon. It may be that the dark background of his theology, to which the mind of this age could not by any effort accommodate itself, threw into greater relief this side of his teaching. The outside darkness of unbelief and irreligion was indeed made very terrible. But the inner world of spiritual experience was wondrous fair. And no human computation will be able to reckon the number of weary toilers in the working and lower middle classes whose narrow surroundings have been brightened and idealised by the glow from the realm of faith to which he introduced them. It was a great thing which this man achieved, to convince multitudes of struggling people, in the midst of a life which everything outward tended to belittle, that their character and career were a matter of infinite concern to the Power who made them, that they could not afford to treat sin lightly, or to throw themselves away as though they were of no account.

The Anglo-Saxon race is not oratorical by temperament; but it has produced orators, and Mr. Spurgeon was in their foremost rank. Preachers of all denominations have found in

him a model of what utterance should be, to
produce the maximum of popular effect. We
are not sure if the greatest profiter by this
form of his example has not been the Anglican
Establishment. It is easy to recognise, in the
free and impassioned utterance, without assist-
ance from manuscript, which has made the
reputation of some Episcopalian preachers, the
leader whom, remote enough from them in
ecclesiastical affinities, they have in this
respect, to their own great advantage, elected
to follow.

And yet at this moment the reflection forces
itself, whether Mr. Spurgeon did not limit his
influence by too great a devotion to the pulpit.
He might have lived longer and worked over
wider areas had he preached less and organised
more. He has died at fifty-eight. Wesley
saw his eightieth year. And to-day the influence of the Methodist leader, a century
after his death, works more effectively than
ever. Great preacher that he was, he understood that to create machinery is better than to
be oneself the sole machine. The founder of
 institutions survives the orator. The effective
force of a Chrysostom is surpassed by a Loyola,
and a General Booth may have proved wiser
in his generation than the pastor of the
Tabernacle. It is true that he did organise,
and effectively. But he was too lavish of

himself. He did prodigies with his individual bow and spear, but great leaders are better employed in creating armies and filling them with their spirit than by exhibiting wonders of individual strength and prowess.

The death of Mr. Spurgeon may be said to close an epoch. The last quarter of a century has seen the forms of religious thinking undergoing profound modification—a process against which he threw the whole weight of his influence. That he was in this respect conscious of fighting a losing battle added something of sadness, and at times of extreme bitterness, to his later utterances. In his fight against the results of Biblical criticism he was seconded by no name of real authority. And there is no one left to whom the world listens to carry on the war. It will not, however, be his attitude in the so-called Down-Grade controversy that will be remembered, any more than Mr. Bright will be thought of in connection with his position on the Irish question. It will be as the preacher who, with unequalled power and success, delivered the Gospel to his generation; as the honest Englishman, whose character, during forty years of unexampled popularity, never swerved from its simplicity and integrity; as the lover of his kind, who opened his heart to the cry of the widow and the orphan, and gave lavishly of his substance to every good work; as the orator who, before such masses of men as no other speaker could statedly command, displayed the strength, the richness, and the persuasive power of the English tongue; as the genuine Christian who, in a materialistic age, set his fellows the example of a piety without ostentation, of a faith without fanaticism, and of an inner life intense without being morbid, that the memory of Charles Haddon Spurgeon will be cherished by his fellow-countrymen.

GOOD FRIDAY AND EASTER DAY.

(A PASSION WEEK MEDITATION.)

SAID Carlyle to Emerson, as once they sat together watching a prospect which.included a distant church spire, "Strange, is it not, that Christ's death at Jerusalem built yonder church?" That event in far-off A.D. 30 will this week occupy the thoughts of millions of minds. The heart of the best part of the world is still in Jerusalem. As an actual city of to-day it has few attractions. Its streets are narrower and dirtier even than those of the average Eastern town. The spectacle of the jostling crowds which, on the great religious anniversaries, represent their rival and bitterly-opposed creeds, is not inspiring. It may be that, before long, the screech of the locomotive and the complete modernisation of the place will profane it more effectually than did the Greek Antiochus when he stood in the holy of holies of its Temple. But there is a Jerusalem other than the one which stands on the Judæan hills, and which

can never be touched by the defiler. It is the
city which lies in the hearts of Christians as the
place of deathless memories. "The Jerusalem
which is from above is free, which is the mother
of us all." When Newman saw Rome he felt
that Oxford was eclipsed. The City of the
Tombs of the Apostles, of the Appian way
along which St. Paul had walked, and of the
Catacombs, overmastered, in the force of religious association, any English shrine. But in
this respect Jerusalem is greater than Rome.
The seven hills yield to Mount Zion and to
Olivet. For the event there consummated, which
Christendom this week commemorates, is still
making the history of the world. After eighteen
centuries of inquiry and speculation men's gaze
is turned upon it with an interest keener than
ever, and with an emotion as deep and fresh as
that which filled the hearts of the first witnesses.

The science of criticism and the philosophy
of history, changing so greatly, as they have
done, our attitude towards the ancient literatures, have turned their fiercest light upon the
records containing the history of Passion Week
and Eastertide, but without altering substan-
tially the Church's sense of their significance.
It is felt now, as of old, that they are, for one
thing, the story of the gaining a new position
in man's perpetual battle against Death. Previously, the world had made a poor show in the

presence of the dread enemy. The utmost
level it had reached was that of resignation,
and it did not often gain that. The best consolation the philosophy both of the earlier or
later ages has offered was, perhaps, that contained in the saying of La Bruyère, that the
universality of Death was its greatest mitiga-
tion. "Had some been permitted to live while
others died, the bitterness of dying would have
been tenfold augmented."

The average feeling of antiquity reflects
itself in the despair of Cicero at the grave of
his daughter; and in the wail of Anacreon, the
poet of amours and of revelry, who, at the end
of life, bemoans himself thus in his last ode:
"I am no longer young. It is on this account
I groan, for I fear Tartarus, and the abyss of
Hades is horrible." And in modern times, in
the circles where the Christian tradition has
lost its power, the shadow of death falls with
all its melancholy gloom. Pièrre Loti, the
new French Academician, has just published a
book called "The Book of Pity and of Death."
It is an unspeakably mournful dirge, whose
burden is the inevitable passing away of all that
one loves, devoured one after another by the
remorseless destroyer who preys on man. Its
picture of gloom is unrelieved by a ray of hope.

But there is another Book of Pity and of
Death—to wit, the New Testament—whose

finding is very different.   It gives us the record
of infinite Pity stooping unto death, and then
places over against that a wonderful history and
doctrine of Resurrection.   That history and
doctrine have taught men how to die.   The his-
toric saying of Wesley concerning his followers,
" Our people die well," has been true of every
age of Christian faith.   From the holy triumph
of Polycarp, amid the torments of martyrdom,
to the beautiful trust of a Catherine Tait, when
she and her husband, the future Archbishop,
in their fever-stricken home at Carlisle, yielded
to God, one after another, five lovely children,
without one doubt as to their Lord's goodness
or the blessedness of their loved ones being
permitted to enter their bleeding hearts, the light
that was kindled in Christ's tomb has not failed.

The import of the death at Jerusalem as a
sacrifice is also fully recognised by the Church
of to-day.   That death was marvellously timed.
Outsiders may call it a coincidence, or a plain
sequence of perfectly natural events, which
made the drama of the Crucifixion to fall in
Passover week, the week in which the Jewish
system of sacrifice had its great and crowning
celebration.   But the Christian instinct, which
found in this fact a profound and world-wide
significance, which held this death as an illustration for all time of sacrifice in its highest
form, and saw in the victim " the Lamb slain

from the foundation of the world," is one which no subsequent findings, either of science, of philosophy, or of criticism, have availed to shake. And the death was followed by a resurrection. Of its mode, of what may be called its natural history, we know nothing. But as a power, the resurrection is operating to-day as distinctly and as evidently as any force in Nature. As certainly as the inscrutable force around us in this glad Springtime is making a new world of life and beauty, so the resurrection power of the Crucified made, and is making, a new world in the sphere of morals and of the spiritual order.

To Goethe the proof of the divineness of Christianity lay in its treatment of the weak, the lowly, and the downtrodden. Heine expressed a similar thought when he said Christianity was the religion of sorrow. The world needs such a religion, for it is full of the weak, and very full of sorrow. The sun rises every day upon multitudes whose inner gloom its brightest rays can neither penetrate nor chase away. Growth is ever through suffering. No great cause comes to birth without pangs of travail. No nation has struggled to its feet without shedding of patriot blood; no house has been without its skeleton, and no heart without its bitterness. This great army of the suffering has been drawn to the Cross as to a magnet,

and they have found in it a marvellous power
of healing. The Divine pity that has looked
upon them from it has drawn the sting from
their wounds. The Great Sufferer has proved
the Great Healer. Calvary has ever been the
refuge of great souls with lost causes.
Athanasius, wandering in the Thebaid, pursued
by an Emperor's wrath; Chrysostom, exiled
from Church and work, dying in the wintry
snows of Pontus; Savonarola, his life-work a
wreck, and his body in the hands of the exe-
cutioners; Mazzini, a fugitive, his country
enslaved, and a price set upon his head, turned
instinctively in thought to Him who from His
Cross looked seemingly also upon a lost cause.
They felt, as all fighters for the right have a
right to feel, that that mighty "stoop to
conquer," which by death opened a kingdom of
heaven to man, is the eternal illustration of the
dynamic truth, that as in nature no atom of
matter or moment of force is ever lost, so no
pain of sacrifice, no moment of endurance for
the truth's sake, but shall find, here or somewhere, its equivalent in high result.

Good Friday is followed by Easter Day.
Hard by the Cross is the open tomb. The
Church is built, not upon death, but upon life.
It could no more subsist upon dead tradition
than spring could be made with the leaves of
last autumn. As to the ultimate fact lying

behind the phenomena of life, whether in a microbe or in the highest development of spiritual consciousness, we have as yet almost everything to learn. The Christian Church cannot explain the mysteries behind its own existence. Sufficient that it still throbs with life, and that it still accounts for that life in the salutation with which the Russian peasant greets his neighbour on Easter Day: " Christ is risen ! "

VOLTAIRE.*

In his "Horæ Sabbaticæ" Sir James Stephen says of Voltaire that he "has perhaps earned a greater amount of fame amongst those who have never read a line of his works than any author of modern times." The truth of this criticism is probably understated. For his fame extends not only amongst those who have never read a line of his works, but who know next to nothing of his real character and of the facts of his career. This is especially the case with the English public, who, as a rule, have very pronounced sentiments on the subject of this work, without possessing about him the veriest minimum of actual information. Not that English literature has neglected Voltaire. Translations of his principal works have appeared at intervals, from the time of Smollett downwards. And the last twenty years have seen the publication of Sir E. Hamley's "Voltaire," of Parton's "Life" in

* Life of Voltaire. By Francis Espinasse. The "Great Writers" Series.

two volumes, and of the elaborate and brilliant study of Mr. John Morley. That, despite these endeavours to enlighten the English people, there remains room for further effort appears from the fact that we heard quite recently a popular preacher quote the phrase "*Écrasez l'Infame*," on the supposition that the "*Infame*" referred to by Voltaire was Jesus Christ.

The present work is confined within certain well-defined limits. The author sets himself to tell the story of his hero's life. He makes no attempt to analyse or to pass a critical judgment upon his literary work. Indeed, in a book of 200 pages, which has for its principal business to trace a most remarkable and varied career, stretching over eighty-three years, to have endeavoured, besides, to discuss from a critical standpoint the works of an author who published over one hundred and fifty volumes in prose and verse, dealing with almost every conceivable subject of human thought, would have been only to court failure. Without any philosophical endeavours to account for Voltaire, to trace the previous evolution of life and thought which made him possible, M. Espinasse plunges at once into his story, which he tells in an eminently bright and readable manner. The successive phases of the poet's strange career, which, beginning six years before the close of the seventeenth century, lasted to the seventy-

eighth year of the eighteenth, his Jesuit education, the development of the dangerous talent
for satire which, exercised in lampooning the
Regent, gave him at twenty-three an acquaintance with the interior of the Bastille; the well-
known quarrel with the Chevalier de Rohan,
when the satirist received a caning at the hands
of the aristocrat; his three years in England,
and the profound impression produced on him
by Locke, Bolingbroke, and Pope; his successful financial operations, which made him probably the wealthiest man of letters who ever
lived; his connection with Madame du Châtelet,
the three years at Berlin with Frederick the
Great, his Ferney life, the apotheosis of the
poet when the Paris population at the Comédie
Française crowned him with laurel and paid
him royal, almost divine, honours, and the
actual as opposed to the apocryphal story of
his death, are told here in a manner which
holds the attention to the end.

When from the modern standpoint we come
to the study of this man and his work, it is
difficult to comprehend the notion which for so
long has ruled concerning Voltaire, that he was
a purely destructive force in the sphere of
morals and religion. It is much easier to
understand the criticism passed on him by an
atheistic reviewer of one of his works—" *C'est
un bigot. Il est déiste.*"

It is true that he attacked Christianity, that he attacked it vehemently, and sometimes with execrable taste. But we have to remember the kind of Christianity he had before his eyes. It was a system which, in his native land, allowed profligates of family, who had spent a youth in debauchery, to be advanced to bishoprics by the intrigues of their mistresses, which ground the faces of the poor, which permitted the infamies of the *corvée* and of the *"droit du Seigneur,"* which repressed all freedom of opinion, and which in his own lifetime had broken men on the wheel for supposed heterodoxy. No great wonder is there that a soul in love with liberty and hating oppression of every kind, should find itself in fierce revolt against a system which seemed identified with all this, and that the wrath which had been aroused in it should have failed to discern between the corruptions of the Gospel and its essence.

That he entirely missed the real significance of Christianity, and that his views of its origin, its early successes and final establishment in the world are to the last degree unphilosophical and impossible, is now recognised by all competent students. It is equally true that in the war he waged against what he regarded as superstition he stooped to ribaldries unworthy of his genius. And yet Voltaire had his religion, which he stoutly maintained and sincerely believed. The church which he built at Ferney, with the inscription, "*Deo Erexit Voltaire*," was by no means a monument of hypocrisy. He was a convinced Theist, believing in a righteous God and in a life to come. His poem on "The Earthquake at Lisbon" is the utterance of a modern Job, with a spirit overwhelmed by the mysteries of life, and yet refusing to let go of faith and resignation. The spirit of true piety breathes in these lines:

La nature est muette, on l'interroge en vain;
On a besoin d'un Dieu qui parle au genre humain:
Il n'appartient qu' a lui d'éxpliquer son ouvrage
De consoler le faible et d'éclairer le sage.

* * * * *

Humble dans mes soupirs, soumis dan ma souffrance
Je ne m'élève point contre la Providence.

That he was able to appreciate a reasonable religion when he met with it is shown by the impression made on him by the religious life of England. He thus describes an interview with a well-known Quaker at Hampstead. "He received me with his hat on, and came towards me without the slightest inclination of the body; but there was more politeness in his frank and benevolent countenance than in our fashion of drawing one leg behind the other, and carrying in the hand what was made to cover the head."

Speaking of the religious toleration characteristic of England he observes : " One goes
to have himself baptized in the name of the
Father, through the Son, and to the Holy
Ghost; another to have his son circumcised,
and some words in Hebrew which he does not
understand muttered over the infant; while a
third betakes himself to his meeting-house, to
wait for the inspiration of God, with his hat
on his head—and all are content. If in England there were only one religion, its despotism
would be to be dreaded; if there were only two
their followers would cut each other's throats;
but there are thirty of them, and they live in
peace and happiness." The last sentence of
this curious passage may well be studied by the
ecclesiastics who are so desirous to-day of
welding the religious life of England into one
organic union.

A phase of Voltaire's work which our
countrymen in their estimate of him are apt to
leave out of sight is that in which he acted as
interpreter, to France and the Continent, of
English philosophy, literature, and scientific
discovery. In philosophy he was a disciple of
Locke and Bolingbroke. He was a great
admirer of Pope, whose " Essay on Man " inspired his own " Discours en vers sur l'Homme."
It was he who made Milton and Shakespeare
known to his countrymen, and who expounded

and defended, in the teeth of strong prejudices, the system of Sir Isaac Newton.

The charge of indecency is brought against him as a writer of comedy, and undoubtedly works like *La Pucelle*, to say nothing of his way sometimes of treating religious questions, form an outrage on propriety. But he is not so gross as his contemporary, Dean Swift, and it is he who, writing of our Wycherley, declares that "he is too indecent for the French." It must never be omitted from our view of him that throughout his life he declaimed with tongue and pen against every species of tyranny and oppression, and was ever ready to sacrifice time, money, and energy in the cause of help-less people whom he believed to be wronged. His conduct in the affair of the Calas family, whose head, a Protestant of blameless character, was done judicially to death at the instigation of a Catholic mob, and in which Voltaire laboured unceasingly, and lavished money, until the innocence of the family was proved and restitution made, gave him the gratitude of the Protestant world. His humanitarian instincts as well as his business capacity were shown in the refugee colony he established at Ferney, where watch-making and silk weaving were carried on with a success which made it one of the most prosperous industrial centres in Europe.

In this article we have followed the example of the biography before us, and have dealt with the man rather than his writings. But the author who, in history, produced the Charles the Twelfth and " Peter the Great," in criticism gave us " The Essay on European Epic Poetry," in tragedy Œdipe and Zaïre, the Henriade in heroic poetry, and in philosophy the Dictionnaire Philosophique, to say nothing of the innumerable other works on all subjects which flowed from that tireless pen, revealed therein an intellect whose versatility, level of performance, and influence over all the contemporary spheres of thought and life, secure it against all detraction as one of the prime forces of the eighteenth century.

BUNYAN AS A CLASSIC.

THAT the Baptist tinker, who suffered years of imprisonment at the hands of the Established Church for unlicensed preaching and the holding of conventicles, should now have his works published at the Clarendon Press of that Oxford University which has been always regarded as the centre of Anglican authority and chief opponent of all ecclesiastical irregularities, may be taken as a measure, not only of Bunyan's literary claims, but also of the distance in the matter of literary and theological judgments which lies between his age and ours. It took a long time for Bunyan to be recognised as an English classic. His first audiences were mainly of the kitchen, and it needed more than one generation to enable society to make up its mind that he was possible in the drawing-room. The common people had long recognised him as the great dramatist of their religious life before Macaulay's brilliant essay, by putting upon him the hall-mark of critical appreciation, made fashionable people willing to avow themselves amongst his admirers. To-day no one disputes his right to share with Milton the title of the prophet-poet of Puritanism. The one has thrown its religious system into an epic, in which the loftiest imaginative genius is allied to encyclopædic learning. The other has made the soul's inner life the theme of a series of dramatic presentations which, unaided as they are by any study of classic models or by any considerable acquaintance with general literature, remain, for their freshness, their actuality, their vivid bodying forth of inner spiritual conditions in terms of external life, unique in the history of religious teaching, while occupying a place apart in the domain of imaginative literature.

The use of allegory as a vehicle for conveying religious ideas is, of course, as old almost as religion itself. Seneca and Cicero apologise for the fables of their classic mythology as forms in which religious truths are at once outlined and veiled. The Brahmans of India make a similar claim for the stories about Vishnu and Siva. In Christian literature, one of the earliest works extant after the apostolic age, the "Shepherd of Hermas," is a curious, though it must be admitted a somewhat weak, specimen of the allegoric style. The notion of the inner life as a pilgrimage has been present in various forms to ecclesiastical writers of every age. Bonaventura suggests it in his "Seven Roads of Eternity." Outside the Church, Lucian uses the idea in the famous sceptical allegory, in which he sets forth the kingdom of truth as inaccessible because of the multitude of cross roads, and of guides who offer contradictory directions.

The mystery plays of the Middle Ages, in which hell and heaven were represented, the one by a big hole at the back of the scaffold, down which the personators of devils and of the wicked were somewhat roughly precipitated, and the other by a raised platform on which men and boys in white robes stood for saints and angels, may be said to have been an anticipation, in a ruder and more concrete form, of Bunyan's Christian dramas. Nothing, however, that had been done in this department previously detracts in the slightest degree from the prodigious originality and marvellous creative power displayed in these works. It is improbable that in writing them the author consulted any authorities except his Bible, his own heart, and the daily life about him. That life was a very strenuous one all round, and it is here vividly reflected. "The Pilgrim's Progress," as well as "The Holy War," is a book of combats. The journey it describes is one in which the hero meets a foe at every other corner, and in which shrewd blows are being exchanged on every possible occasion.

The Englishman, it may be said, is a born fighter, and rather likes taking his religion in this fashion. Bunyan, moreover, had been through the Parliamentary wars, and had handled a pike himself. To a contemporary of the Ironsides it was natural that theological ideas should shape themselves in martial forms. But it was surely of the inspired genius that was in him that, while fascinating youth and age alike by his stirring battle-pieces, he should teach the world that the most real history of all that is transacted on this planet is that in which the combats delivered are not with blare of trumpet and roar of cannon, but silent, in the viewless realms within, where the soul of man struggles against the brute in him, where the victories are of faith against doubt, of spirit against flesh, of conscience and the sense of duty against self-indulgence.

Of his two principal works, " The Holy War " is as far inferior to " The Pilgrim's Progress " as is " Paradise Regained " to " Paradise Lost," or Goethe's continuation of *Faust* to the original drama. The theme itself does not offer the possibilities of its great rival. The journey of the " Progress " carries us over new ground at every step, abounds in incident, and ends in a consummation worthy of what has gone before. The War is, on the contrary, confined to one spot, and has a *dénouement* which lacks finality. The characters in the latter work are unsubstantial. We find it impossible to fall in love with Captain Boanerges, or Mr. Conscience, as we do with Christian, Faithful, Mr. Greatheart, or old Mr. Honest. The teaching, too, is, a good deal of it, entirely unpalatable to the modern mind. Shaddai is, one feels, a very arbitrary monarch, who fails, somehow, to commend his sayings and doings to our sense of right; and some of the answers to the arguments of Diabolus are, alas! by no means satisfactory. "Mansoul," in the nineteenth century, would not be disposed to capitulate to the assault of Captain Boanerges, whose "scutcheon was the three burning Thunderbolts," or to Ensign Terror, who "bare the red colours, and his scutcheon was a burning fiery furnace."

Nevertheless, the work is a wonderful one, and had the "Pilgrim's Progress" never been written, would doubtless have been regarded as a masterpiece of allegorising. It analyses with marvellous acuteness the twists and turns of human thought and desire, and there are hits at the then existing state of society as caustic in their satire as anything in Juvenal. The English is that of our Bible, having the same sinewy Saxon strength, the same fresh aroma of the olden time.

One of the things which the spiritual consciousness of the age may be expected before long to evolve will be a nineteenth or twentieth century Bunyan, with a new allegory, in which the elements of thought, feeling, and external environment which enter into the modern religious position will, as in that of the tinker, be clothed for us in forms of living reality. An immense literary success is within reach of the man who could do for the inner life of to-day what the dreamer of two centuries ago did for that of his generation. If Mr. Stead ever gets committed to prison again, his good genius ought to put him into a trance where he may dream a Pilgrim's Progress for our time.

THE RELIGIOUS ROGUE.

"THE City is full of cheating," said once, from a metropolitan pulpit, a distinguished preacher since dead. To the lips of many profane persons, if they had heard this attack, would have leaped the rejoinder, "Yes, and the biggest cheats of all are your religious men." The sentiment expressed here is unquestionably a widely-spread one, and some recent events in the world of finance have caused its repetition in many circles with an added accent of cynicism. It is worth while to inquire into the feeling, and to ascertain, if possible, what amount of truth lies at the bottom of it. The religious rogue undoubtedly exists, and what we are greatly in need of is an accurate natural history of him. He has figured in history, and very prominently in literature. But we do not know of any really successful attempt to account for him as a human phenomenon. We meet him early. He appears in the New Testament as the gentleman who makes long prayers and who varies these exercises by devouring widows' houses. Boccaccio, Chaucer, and the author of "Litteræ Obscurorum Virorum," whoever he was, have painted him for us as the rascally, libidinous monk who used his profession as a cloak for all manner of villainies. Molière has given us Tartuffe, and Dickens has made the character odious as Pecksniff and ridiculous as Chadband. We have laughed at the religious rogue in fiction, and loathed him in history and actual life, without, perhaps, having carefully analysed the elements in his composition, or examined, with any approach to philosophy, his actual significance as related to religion.

The character we are studying may be roughly defined as a person who, while making an active religious profession, outrages morality in some one or other of its forms. In applying this definition, however, we find ourselves at the outset compelled to make an important distinction. When we talk about outraging morality we are reminded that the moral standard has been a variable quantity in different ages. Any one, for instance, who spoke of the patriarchs as religious rogues would show an utter lack of fairness and of historical sense. Yet, according to the Biblical record, these pioneers of faith and religion conducted themselves in a manner which, in the England of the nineteenth century, would assuredly have landed

11

them in gaol at an early date. The seeming anomaly is explained by the primitive social code of the time they lived in.

This relation of character to the current standard of morality must never be forgotten in our judgment of individuals. To take an illustration nearer our own day, it would be absurd to question the religious sincerity or the general character of George Whitfield or of John Newton. Yet the one purchased slaves in Georgia, and the other, for a time after his conversion, was the captain of a slave ship. Phenomena of this kind are all over the field of history, and the explanation is that the religious consciousness had not, in these cases, reached its present clearness of vision and of affirmation on special points of social morality.

When we come to the character which genuinely answers to our definition, to the commonly recognised religious rogue, we find his presence in society resulting from two main causes, which may be taken as, in their operation, dividing the *genus* we are studying into two different species. The first of these is the conjunction of a real religious feeling with a meagre or undeveloped moral sense. We have all of us laughed at the man in the mulberry suit whom Mr. Sam Weller found shedding copious tears over his hymn-book, and who succeeded in completely taking in that

usually astute individual. What Dickens, however, fails to note is that this worthy's predilec-
tion for hymns and hymn-books might have been
real, without in any way interfering with his
essential rascality. He would be a very super-
ficial student of human nature who should
assert that because Henry VIII. developed into
a monster of blood and lust, his position as a
defender of theological orthodoxy was a mere
pretence. He would be equally so who denied
real fervour to the religious exercises of those
Sicilian bandits who practise all the rites of
their Church, but who pillage and, on occasion,
assassinate the travellers who fall into their
hands. There are, too, in our present-day
western communities, men of imaginative temperament who can be excited to the highest
pitch by emotional religious worship, but who
are not to be trusted in matters of conduct. In
all these cases we are in contact, not with pretence or hypocrisy, but with a want of assimila-
tion of the moral ideas which religion holds in
solution. These people find in religion affinities
with their imaginative and sentimental side,
but have little or no response to its ethical
teaching. When this class is numerous in a
so-called Christian community, it points to the
fact that the institutions and services of the
Church have been used there rather for the
excitement of feeling than for the enlighten-

ment of the conscience and for the definite training of character.

There are, however, as we have already contended, religious rogues with a different history from this behind them, and a different set of causes operating towards their production. These are men who began life with a genuine spiritual enthusiasm, accepting Christianity not only as an emotional inspiration, but as an ethical discipline. For years they could be counted on as sound, not only in the faith, but also in character. All was well with them until they found themselves crossing that part of the life-journey which in a previous chapter we have designated as "the Dangerous Years." It was when well on in middle life, when religious exhortations, by their very frequency, had lost force; when an increasing position had awakened an appetite for self-indulgence and for the wealth which secures it, while weakening the desire for spiritual satisfactions; when an ever-widening contact with the world had made them familiar with, and tolerant of, moral standards which in earlier days would have shocked and repelled them; when other men's defalcations and dishonesties towards themselves had filled them with cynicism and bitterness, that they arrived at a moral crisis which many, thank God, come victoriously through, but which in some cases eventuates in the production of our second class of religious rogue.

It is a strange and terrible irony of circumstance that often in these histories the earlier religious career comes to be, in a sense, the instrument of downfall. While the ethical steadfastness of men of this kind has been declining, their reputation as persons of standing in the Church has been widening, and has secured for them and their enterprises a public confidence which could not otherwise have been reckoned upon. People trust them unlimitedly with their money, with their goods, with the conduct of their affairs. They awake some morning to discover that the reputation on which they had staked so much is entirely unsupported by character, while the outside world finds a new text on which to discourse concerning the hollowness of religious profession in general.

And yet these men are not like Bulstrode, whom George Eliot depicted in " Middlemarch," who was a fraud from the beginning. They were genuine once. But their ethical nature had no " deepness of earth," and so, under the scorching heat of the later life surroundings, " it withered away." The history is humiliating, but the lesson from it is salutary. *Obsta Principiis* ("Resist the beginnings"), the motto of one of our Oxford Colleges, is a precept for more than undergraduates. If we would escape the precipice, we must learn to recognise at sight the point where the level ceases and the incline begins. And we must, in the fulness and complexities of our mid-career, still commence each day with the prayer we learned in childhood at our mother's knee, "Lead us not into temptation, but deliver us from evil."

LUCIAN :

LUCIAN is sometimes spoken of as one of the early opponents of Christianity. Whether he may be with correctness thus designated is a matter of some controversy, about which we shall have something to say later. But apart from his relation to the Christian Church, there is to the student something peculiarly interesting in the career and in the utterance of this great heathen writer of the second century. The manifold genius of the man, his immense erudition, the Attic grace of his style, which recalls the golden age of Greek literature, his versatility, now in his reckless gaiety and merciless satire reminding us of Aristophanes, and again, by his penetrating analysis of the most complicated philosophical problems, seeming to make Socrates speak again—all this draws us to him. But what, after all, most enchains us is the vivid picture his writings give of the life and manners of that strange time. We have brought before us, as though an electric light had been turned on the picture, the whole phantasmagoria of that Greek-Roman civilisation in its period of decay. We see there the morbid symptoms of it, the utter bewilderment of opinion, with the old beliefs gone and no new ones to take their place, the shameless profligacy, the intolerable airs of the wealthy, and the ridiculous antics of the social parasites who surrounded them, the contemptible hypocrisy of the swarms of sophists who, themselves utterly vicious, made a market of their professions of virtue, and here and there the pathetic struggles of some nobler spirit, a Nigrerius or a Demonax striving amid the prevailing corruption to carve out for himself some semblance of a nobler life. It may be worth our while to try and place ourselves, if only for a moment, at the mental standpoint of Lucian, this man who, with a luminous intellect, versed in all the literature of his time, seeking for himself to penetrate the mystery of life, finds nothing in the accepted religion of his country but a collection of childish superstitions, in philosophy only the clash of warring sects, and pretensions which disappear at the first touch of criticism, and to whom Christianity meant only the faint rumour about a bizarre cult of some obscure people not worthy the attention of a thinker. The interest with which we

study such a mental interior is not simply historical. For we see in what passed in this
man's mind the reflection of very much that is
found in the educated intellect of to-day. It
is, in fact, from the close resemblance of many
of the phenomena, intellectual and moral, of
the second century, as revealed in Lucian's
pages, with those of the nineteenth, and the
message of warning which these phenomena of
the earlier age bring to us of the later, that
such a study as this seems to us to derive its
value.

Lucien was a native of Samosata, a town on
the Euphrates. His birth, the exact date of
which is not known with precision, is supposed
to have taken place at the end of the reign of
Adrian, or at the beginning of that of Antoninus
Pius—from 137 to 140 A.D. After leaving
school, as he tells us in "The Dream"—a work
from which we get some interesting biographical details—he was placed first with an
uncle who was a sculptor. He gives us a
lively account of this first attempt to establish
him. Having had the misfortune to break the
tablet of marble which had been given him for
the purpose of making his first essay, his new
master caught up a strap and inflicted on him
a severe chastisement. Smarting from his
wounds, he fled home and told to his indignant
mother the story of his ill-treatment. That

night, he says, he had a dream which decided his destiny. Two female figures stood before him, the one representing Sculpture, and the other Knowledge. The first, who had a rough exterior with the dress and manner of the working class, told him if he would give himself to her, he should do work as great as that of Phidias or Praxiteles, and that men should worship as gods the offspring of his skill. The other figure, who was beautifully dressed and had a noble and engaging air, then spoke in a way which gives us a curious idea of the social estimation in which a sculptor was at that time held. "Follow Sculpture," says she, "and you will be after all only a workman, receiving a trifling emolument, isolated from all, a man lost in the crowd, on your knees before the great. Though you should become a Phidias and produce a thousand *chefs d'œuvre* it will be your art and not you that men will praise." She then proceeds to enlarge on the fortune and renown that await him if he follows herself. He will be loaded with honours, ranked among the noblest; every one who meets him will point him out to his neighbour and say, "That is he." After this he bade adieu to sculpture and, as an introduction to letters, entered on the career of an advocate in the tribunals of Antioch. But he had not yet found his true vocation. The "gentlemen of

the long robe," who in most times appear to
have had a somewhat sinister reputation,
receive anything but a flattering character
from Lucian. According to him, knavery,
lying, impudence, brawling, and bawling were
amongst the regular tools and stock-in-trade of
the profession. He left it to become a professional rhetorician. It was in this line of things
that his genius immediately declared itself. In
those days the orator was in immense vogue.
The Empire seems to have been an even better
hunting-ground for the travelling lecturer than
America is to-day. The rhetor, or sophist,
arriving at a town in Gaul or Italy or Syria,
announced an oration, and, if he had any
reputation, he was sure of a crowd who paid
handsomely for the treat he had given them.
Lucian followed this career for some time with
splendid success, traversing Ionia, Achaia,
Macedonia, Italy, and Gaul. During this
period he took up his abode for a time at Athens,
in order to perfect himself in his Greek studies.
From there he proceeded to Rome, where he
made the acquaintance of the philosopher
Nigrerius, whom he has immortalised in his
work of that name. Having now become rich,
he made a second sojourn at Athens, enjoying
the society of Demonax, of whom he has given
us a striking eulogium, and whose life of lofty
simplicity stands out in striking contrast to that

of the horde of greedy adventurers who usurped
and disgraced the name of philosophy. It was
now, having reached his fortieth year, and when
his mind was at the height of its analytic and
creative force, that, applying himself to the
serious study of philosophy, he began to produce the works which have immortalised him.
He had previously gained the ear of his
contemporaries. He now spoke to all time.
Become one of the most illustrious men of the
age, he made a visit to his native town of
Samosata, where he had a splendid reception.
Some time after this he obtained an important
post in the imperial administration in Egypt.
He lived to an advanced age, dying, it is stated,
of an attack of gout.

Let us now see some of the things this man
had to say to the world. In the necessarily
meagre and imperfect sketch, which is all we
can give here, we will endeavour briefly to
indicate his attitude to the paganism of the
time, to its philosophy, to its social conditions,
and finally, his position with reference to
Christianity.

As to the first point, no better evidence
could be adduced of the universal decay of faith
in the gods of Olympus than the writings of our
author. That a man who used such licence of
language with reference to the national religion
should have enjoyed, as he did, the highest

consideration with both rulers and people, shows the striking change which had come over the minds of men with reference to the ancient divinities. At an earlier period such utterances would infallibly have brought upon him the fate of Socrates. In his " Dialogues of the Gods " he brings on to his stage, one after another, the whole Olympian troupe, and exhibits them in *rôles* as absurd as that of the traditional policeman in a Christmas pantomime. In " Jupiter Confounded " he delivers a more serious attack. Taking up the received mythology, he proves that, on its own showing, the gods, with Jupiter at their head, are impotent and insignificant, seeing it is by the Parcæ, the fateful sisters who spin or cut the thread of destiny, that all affairs in heaven and earth are, in the long run, decided. In his work on " Sacrifices," after holding up to ridicule the methods adopted in different countries for propitiating their deities, he thus concludes : " All this superstition accepted by the vulgar mind has, in my view, less need of a censor than of a Democritus or an Heraclitus, the one to laugh at the folly of men, the other to weep over their ignorance."

But if this keen intellect can find no path to truth along the line of the old traditions, what has he to say of the philosophy in vogue amongst the learned ? His verdict here is not a whit more favourable. Perhaps his most important and suggestive deliverance on this subject is found in his "Hermotimus or the Sects." In this famous dialogue he introduces a devoted adherent of the Stoic school, who has for many years devoted all his time and energy and fortune to the business of gaining the "sovereign good" by philosophy. A friend, Lycernis, enters into controversy with him, and, using the Socratic method, begins to push him with embarrassing questions. In answering them he is obliged to confess that he has not yet attained what he seeks, and that to do so will take him many years at his present rate of progress. "But has his favourite teacher attained it himself? If so, how comes it that one who should be free from avarice, from anger, from the grosser appetites, is one about whom proofs to the contrary are so numerous? Then why is he sure that the Stoic philosophy is the true one? Are there not many other systems—the Peripatetic, the Platonist, the Epicurean, the Pythagorean? Do not these differ in vital points? In order to pronounce as to which of these is true it will be necessary, will it not, to study them thoroughly; and as to become a proficient in any one of them requires, according to their own account, at least twenty years, how long must a man live before he has found out which

way to follow? If it be said that at the outset
he must make a choice of guides, the question
comes, How is he to know who are the true
guides? Who is to direct his choice? If he
take the testimony of others, will. he not
require testimony about these others, and so
ad infinitum? " In a striking passage our
author then pictures Virtue as a kind of
celestial city, to which men need to make a
sort of pilgrim's progress. The inhabitants
are none of them born in the city, but are
immigrants from other lands. The conditions
of entrance are that a man have intelligence,
the love of goodness, the scorn of low delights,
a soul which shows no yielding to the difficulties
to be encountered on the way thither. In
reading this one might imagine we had before
us a page of Bunyan. But in what follows
there creeps out our author's scepticism—a
scepticism which is the more mournful since it
seems forced upon him, spite of his yearning
for the higher life. "Alas!" says he, "in
setting out for this city one encounters a crowd
of men who profess to be guides. But the
roads by which they propose to conduct you are
not the same. They run in opposite directions.
Some lead East and some West, some take you
through deserts and wildernesses, and others
through gardens of delight. But each competitor declares that he is the proper guide,

and his way the right one." The bewildered
Stoic is thus pushed from point to point till
all his ideas and arguments are shown, one by
one, to be worthless. He weeps in his despair,
exclaiming, "Oh, what have you done to me,
Lycernis? You have reduced my treasure to
ashes. I have lost, I see it too clearly, all my
years and my painful endeavours." In the
end Lycernis, the questioner, recommends him
to "determine henceforth to live like the rest
of the world, instead of pursuing foolish hopes
and ambitious ideas." And Hermotimus goes
away with the determination to give up everything—the special garb he had worn, his
studies, his severity of life; "and as for
philosophers, if, by chance, and spite of my
precautions, I encounter any of them, I will
get out of their way as though I were running
from a mad dog." From this, at first sight,
we might imagine that Lucian's attitude was
one of universal scepticism, that with him
truth was to be found nowhere, that it was no
use troubling ourselves about the higher
questions of life, and that the true wisdom
was to let everything go, and live as we list.
That, however, would, we believe, be a mis-
conception of his meaning. His hand, it is
true, is against the professed exponents of
truth, but not against the true and good in
itself, or the quest of it. One sentence from

the work we have been quoting gives us, perhaps, the best idea of what he is really driving at:

Evidently you have never reflected that virtue consists principally in acts, in the practice of justice, of wisdom, and of courage. You, on the contrary, and by you I mean the chiefs of the philosophic sects, neglect this practical business, in order to exercise yourselves in syllogisms, in embarrassing questions, in a miserable play upon words, and in these puerilities you take up the greater part of your lives.

What, after all, is this but, in substance, Matthew Arnold's dictum, that conduct is three-fourths of life? That he had a real admiration for goodness when fortunate enough to meet with it, is sufficiently shown by his biographical sketches of Nigrerius and of Demonax, two philosophers with whom successively he had lived on the most intimate terms, with the one at Rome and the other at Athens, and whom he paints as filled with the loftiest ideal of life, scorning riches and all that the world ran after, and occupying themselves with the pursuit of truth and the practice of virtue. And no one can read his noble eulogy of Demosthenes without feeling that his nature had in it quick response to true greatness.

But, unquestionably, the *rôle* of Lucian amongst the schools of philosophy was not so much to ascertain and declare what is true as

12

to unveil error and lash hypocrisy. Never was there a more biting satirist, and never had satirist a richer field for his powers. With the unbridled licence of an Aristophanes, he has also hits so full of the modern spirit that one might fancy we had a Voltaire or a Thackeray talking to us through a telephone across sixteen centuries. Here is a photograph of the Sophists of his day:

There has arisen of late to the surface of society a set of people, idle, quarrelsome, greedy, swollen with insolence—" a useless burden to the earth," as Homer says. These men, having formed themselves into different groups, have invented I know not how many labyrinths of words, and call themselves Stoics, Academicians, Epicureans, Peripatetics, and other names still more ridiculous. Dressing themselves in the respectable garb of virtue, with solemn look and long beard they go about, disguising the infamy of their morals under this taking exterior, like the "supers" at a theatre, all mask and gold-broidered robe, showing, when these are taken off, nothing but a miserable half-sized abortion who gets five shillings for a representation. Getting around them a number of easily duped young men, they declaim to them with a tragic air the commonplaces of morals. In presence of their disciples they laud to the skies temperance and courage, disparaging riches and pleasure, but when left to themselves who can describe their gormandising, their lubricity, their money-grubbing?

Scathing words these, which have been true before now of Christian ecclesiastics as well as

of heathen sophists. In such portraits of the
moral teachers of the age, of which we have
innumerable similar specimens, we are continually reminded of the pictures of the monks
of the Middle Ages given in that book which
has been described as the egg out of which
Luther hatched the Reformation, the " Litteræ
Obscurorum Virorum." To be the professional
exponent of morality is a perilous business,
whether the morality be that of the Bible or of
the Schools. Woe be to society when the work
falls into the hands of the insincere and the
ignoble !

But if at times, as in the passage above
quoted, Lucian pours hot indignation over
these hypocritical teachers, his usual vein is
one of mocking irony. In one of his "Dialogues of the Dead," for instance, he sketches
a company of passengers whom Charon, assisted
as usual by Mercury, is about to ferry across
the Styx. Amongst them is one of our
philosophers. Charon complains that his boat
is old and crazy, and says that to lighten it the
passengers must strip themselves of everything
superfluous. When it comes to the turn of
the philosopher to be examined an amusing
scene commences. Says Mercury, " But who
is this man with the grave demeanour, the
lofty air, and the long beard ? " One replies,
" It is a sophist, Mercury. Strip him, and

you will find some laughable things under his robe." Mercury: " Now, then, take off first this demeanour of yours, and then the other things. By Jupiter, what an amount of brag he has got upon him! What a quantity of ignorance, of chicanery, of captious questions, of thorny discourses, of twisted ideas! But, lo and behold! here are also gold, the taste for illicit pleasures, impudence, anger, luxury, licence. Nothing of all that escapes me, spite of all your efforts to conceal it. Leave here also your lies, your pride, and that idea that you are worth so much more than everybody else. If you get into the boat with all that baggage, what vessel of fifty rowers would be sufficient to receive you ? "

Parenthetically it may here be said that in these " Dialogues of the Dead " we get a curious glimpse into the mental interior of our author on the subject of the future state. The idea is with him absolutely emptied of every element of the serious or the awful. The personages who people the lower world are made to figure as burlesque actors in the comedy of existence. Cerberus, Pluto, Charon, Mercury, and the shades committed to their charge, laugh, crack jokes, and exhibit themselves in absurd situations. The groans even of the rich who find themselves in these gloomy realms despoiled of all, are made to take a comical turn. With this reckless jester life is an extravaganza which is kept up with unabated spirit on both sides the grave.

But, as we have before said, the thing which, perhaps, above all others makes Lucian so interesting to us, is the vivid picture he gives us of the manners of his age. As we read his page the dead and buried century in the midst of which he stood throbs again with life. Under his guidance we find ourselves now at the banqueting table of a Roman noble, with its endless profusion, its crowds of attendant slaves, the haughty airs of the wealthier guests, the forced jests of the social parasite ; or we are strolling down the Ceramicus with the Parthenon at our backs, one of a group of gossiping Greeks who, on their way to the Piræus, are discussing the politics of the hour or chuckling over some choice scandal. We are laughing spite of ourselves at the stupendous effrontery of an Alexander of Abotonichos who, in the art of humbugging a credulous poople, could give points to any Cagliostro or Barnum that modern times have produced. We note in these pictures of society the brilliancy of the varnish that is on the surface of things. We shudder as we gaze into the gulfs of corruption that yawn beneath. What a curious glimpse, for instance, is that given of the morning promenade of a Roman noble who amongst his crowd of

attendants has one whose function it is to
nod for him to passing acquaintances, and
another to inform him when the road goes
down hill and when up!

And could the force of absurdity go further
than in the parasite who, having exhausted
every possible eulogy on his patron, at last,
seeing the latter is troubled with a cough, falls
back on the remark that he spits with a remark-
ably good grace !

One of the most striking of his social
sketches is that in which he depicts the miseries
of those philosophers who consent to enter the
private service of the great. As we read his
description of the position of these unhappy
mortals in noble households, the slights they
received from both master and servants, passed
over at table when the best wines and the most
dainty meats were being served, made to wait
on every whim and caprice of the mistress of
the house, their slender purse exhausted by
gifts to insolent domestics—a blackmail which
they were compelled to pay if they would
receive the smallest service from them—we
seem to forget the lapse of centuries and to
imagine we are listening to the complaint of
some " poor devil " author of the eighteenth
century reciting the humiliations he had to
put up with from his patron, or the shrill tones
of Jean Jacques Rousseau as he exclaims

against the almost precisely similar treatment
he met with in the households of the French
grandees.

With Lucian the rich meet with almost as
severe a handling as the sophists. He is fond
of showing what poor creatures they are, how
absolutely dependent. " Of what use would be
their pomp and magnificence if the poor chose
to withhold the tribute of their admiration
and envy?" He again and again urges the
lesson, which is worth repeating in our own
day, that the poor man, if he will only preserve
the dignity and simplicity of his position, keeping free from envy and being satisfied with
what he has, will have the rich man in his
power, inasmuch as it is only by the admiration
expressed for his magnificence by others that
the latter derives from it any satisfaction or
importance. He is never weary, either, of
painting the disabilities of the rich. Their
splendid banquets bring on a train of diseases,
their possessions make them afraid of every
rumour of war or violence, their heir wishes for
their death, and often helps it forward. Here
is the soliloquy of a wealthy man who is discovered in his house at night with a pale,
anxious face, counting his treasures.

" There, I have seventy talents put in a place of
safety. I have hid them in the ground under my bed
without anybody seeing me. But I am afraid that

rascally groom of mine must have noticed the sixteen talents hid in the stable. Evidently that is why he is now so continually pottering about amongst the horses there, for he is neither careful nor industrious naturally. Unless he has been pilfering, how is it he has been able to lay in all those provisions? And I am told he has just bought his wife a collar of five drachmas. I am a lost man; these scoundrels will ruin me completely. Apropos, my plate is not well concealed, and it is plate of no ordinary kind. Well, the best way is to keep a stout guard. Let us go the round of the house. Who goes there? By Jupiter, I see you, you rascal, trying to get over the wall there! The gods be praised, it is only a pillar!"

Hardly an enviable state of things this, surely! The millionaires of to-day, with their banking facilities and the possibility of solid investments, have certainly a better time of it than their brother of the second century.

It is time, however, to deal with that which, to the Christian thinker, is of critical importance in the writings of Lucian—his relation to the Church. Leaving untouched, as we are compelled to do, much of his most brilliant work, his fine art criticisms, his masterly critical treatise, "How History should be Written," than which surely nothing better on the subject has been or can be said, his works of fanciful imagination, which exhibit him as the Defoe or Jules Verne of his age, let us come now to his attitude to that new religion which, across all the distractions, the scepticisms, the vices of the time, was steadily making its way, destined to swallow up this old order and to create a new one. He has been quoted often as a professed enemy of the Gospel, and has been, in fact, spoken of as an apostate from Christianity. For this latter supposition there is not a shadow of foundation, and that he was a professed opponent of the Church is perhaps more than a cautious writer would be inclined to say. In one direction it is certain that his influence told in favour of it. His merciless ridicule of the old paganism and his keen exposure of the deficiencies of the current philosophy helped to bring on the downfall of both, and so prepared the way for the new faith. There is evidence, in fact, in the writings of both the Greek and the Latin fathers that in their arguments against paganism they borrowed weapons from his arsenal. His personal relation to the Gospel we had best gather from his own utterances. Of the three writings attributed to him which contain direct references to Christianity, the one which takes the form of an open attack, the "Philopatris," is now generally recognised as spurious. It is a stupid and clumsy attempt to pour ridicule on the doctrine of the Trinity and other Christian beliefs, and is evidently the work of a later hand. It has in it some

curious and interesting references. Thus twice
over we have an oath by "the Unknown God
who is adored at Athens." And this passage :
" I met a bald-headed Galilean with a hooked
nose who has been in the third heaven, where
he heard astonishing things. He renews us
by water ; he makes us march in the footsteps
of the blessed, and redeems us from the abode
of the wicked." There is here evidently a
jumble of ideas relating to Paul and to Christ.
The Christians are also sneered at as people
who live in the clouds, expecting nothing but
evil to happen to the world and all who are
in it.

In " Alexander, or the False Prophet," which
is undoubtedly from Lucian's pen, there is a
brief reference to the Christians, where
Alexander complains that Pontus is filled with
Atheists and Christians—an indirect testimony
to the fact that the new doctrine was already
widely spread in Asia Minor. It is, however,
in his account of the death of Peregrinus
that we have the most definite declaration
of our author on the subject of Christianity. Here he has been understood, though
without sufficient foundation, as writing dis-
paragingly of Christian martyrdom. He pours
scorn indeed on Peregrinus and on his death,
which was, in fact, a showy suicide. But
Peregrinus was not a professing Christian at

the time of his death. He had been an
adherent of the Church, but had left it to
join the cynic sect of philosophers, by members
of whom he was surrounded when he mounted
the funeral pyre and made his theatrical exit
from life. The different references in the
Peregrinus to Christ and His followers we give
here word for word. Speaking of Peregrinus
he says, "Many regarded him as a god, a
legislator, a pontiff, equal to him who is
honoured in Galilee, where he was crucified for
having introduced this new cult among men."
Of the Christians he says:

Nothing equals their eagerness to help unfortunate
brethren. . . . These poor people think they will
live eternally. In consequence they scorn punishment,
and deliver themselves freely to death. . . . Their
first legislator has persuaded them they are all
brethren. From the time they change their religion
they renounce the gods of Greece and adore the
Crucified Sophist whose laws they follow. They
despise equally all earthly goods, and live in common,
in the complete faith they have in his words. So that
if a rascal presents himself among them he can enrich
himself quickly, laughing in his sleeve at their
simplicity.

It is easy from these words to gather what his
attitude was to the new religion. It was not
that of active opposition so much as philosophic indifference. He had evidently never
deeply inquired into it. Vague rumours had

reached him of this faith at a time, probably, when his mind had become hardened by the habitual lashing of roguery and superstition into the idea that every new movement was only another illustration of the old wearisome story of man's folly or hypocrisy. And that such a man should have assumed such an attitude as the habitual one of his thinking is, to us, one of the most powerful testimonies to the human need for the Gospel. Lucian had looked into his age to find nothing in it but emptiness and vanity. The spectacle had made him a mocker and a railer. But man cannot live by scorn alone. Human nature can never develop healthily unless, in addition to the lateral look around it, and the downward look on what is beneath it, it has also the upward look to what is above. In other words, human nature must have its ideal, its hero, its object of adoration and of love. What possibilities would have opened in this man's life had he known Christ as Paul knew Him!

And if that is the lesson we draw from the study of Lucien himself, the one which comes from the contemplation of his age is like unto it. In our own day men are proposing to us to give up revealed religion and to rely on philosophy and culture as adequate supports of morality. The age of Lucian gives us, we think, a tolerably clear idea of what would be the results of an experiment of that kind. That age had in its memory the utterances of all the great philosophies. In the fine arts its eye was trained to the nicest appreciation of colour and form. The boasted Greek civilisation had spread all over the empire. But in no time in the history of man has there been, probably, a greater moral turpitude, a more complete bewilderment in face of the enigmas of life, a more utter absence of that moral idea which creates great characters and lifts human nature towards its true destiny. Nowhere than to the writer we have been studying can we go for a better illustration of the truth that man, whether in the individual or collectively as a race, cannot climb to the highest by himself. He must be lifted from above.

MONTAIGNE.

THERE are few writers of the first class about whom more diverse judgments have been formed than Montaigne. A modern critic has declared that his principal characteristic is boundless garrulity, and that he is the father of the race of penny-a-liners. By others he has been extolled as reaching the limits of the possible in human reason. Many, with Pascal, have pronounced him the most dangerous of heretics. Pope Gregory XIII., on the contrary, whom he visited in Rome, warmly commended him for the devotion he had shown to the Church. Whatever opinion we may form as to his merits or demerits, either as a man or as a writer, two things may certainly be predicated of him. He has been to every generation which has succeeded him prodigiously entertaining, and he has exerted an influence of the most important kind upon later European thinking. He and his fellow-countryman, Rabelais, were fellow-workers in the diffusion of this influence, and they are a striking illustration of the truth that

men of genius affect the mind of their contemporaries and descendants, not so much by
the opinions they advance as by the atmosphere
they create. To a generation given up to the
fiercest religious controversy these two men
came with an entirely different message.
The note they struck was that of Pyrrhonism
and Humanism. To the philosophers and
theologians of the time they said in effect,
"What are you all wrangling about? You
and the rest of us know nothing as to ultimate
truth. But we perceive that sugar is sweet
and that good wine refresheth the palate.
Come and let us enjoy ourselves." Born in
the third decade of the sixteenth century, and
writing his essays in the midst of controversies
so fierce that assassinations, Wars of the
League, and Bartholomew massacres were the
expression of the passions excited, our author
chats to us about coaches, of smells, and
concerning the wearing of clothes, retailing
his good things with the air of one to whom
the throat-cutting and town-burning going on
around him, and the causes of all this, were
not worth the trouble even of description.
"I am of a humour," says he, "that, life and
health excepted, there is nothing for which I
will bite my nails, and that I will purchase at
the price of torment of mind and constraint."
The *esprit gaulois*, whether appearing in the

La Fontaine of the first century, the Voltaire
of a second, or the Renan of the third after
Montaigne, the spirit which concludes the
gravest argument with a jest, and hints that the
human drama is probably more of a farce than
anything else, is one for which our essayist,
in conjunction with the author of "Pantagruel," is very largely answerable.

But the essays have done much more than to
create a spirit. They will always be in season
for the information they contain on three interesting subjects—the author, his contemporaries, and the classical and mediæval literature
of which he was a wholesale dealer and general
purveyor. They are, for one thing, a kind of
personal confession. It has been said there is
copy in every man's life, if it could be got at.
There was abundance of copy in Montaigne,
and he has done his best to make it accessible.
He has given us the minutest details of his
bodily appearance, his mental characteristics,
and his daily habits. We learn that he was,
much to his own annoyance, in statue below
the middle height; that, like our Cromwell, he
had "an untuneable voice"; that, as was
Macaulay, he was clumsy to a degree in
physical exercises; and that he wrote a hand
which he often could not himself decipher.
Though singularly daring in speculation, he
confesses, as did Samuel Johnson, to harbouring

a few superstitions in small matters. "I think myself excusable if I prefer the odd number; Thursday rather than Friday; if I had rather be the twelfth or fourteenth than the thirteenth at table." The man who seems in his works to have the whole of classical literature at his fingers' ends assures us that he had absolutely no memory. Like Sydney Smith, he was in danger at times of forgetting his own name. To remember anybody else's was entirely beyond him.

In religious matters he expresses himself ordinarily as a devout Catholic, but passages in his essays here and there enable us to see what this profession really amounted to. The sum is that, as we really know nothing absolutely, it is best to accept the existing religion as a sufficient working hypothesis. Morality is an affair of climate and custom, what one nation abhors being held by another in high respect and esteem. We are in this world like a man pushing his way through a crowd, where his course is determined not merely by his own motion, but by that of the people around, who push and press him this way and that. Montaigne might, indeed, be called the father of French Opportunism. Views of this kind may seem largely flavoured with cynicism, but there were many qualities in him which make him estimable and in a way lovable. He abhorred lying and pretence of every kind. He was eminently humane, both in theory and conduct. His essay on the education of children reveals not only the clearness of his insight, but a capacity for genuine and warm affection. Few better things have been said on the subject before or since.

We go to Montaigne, however, not only for the self-revelation of a singularly full and interesting mind, but for the vivid light he casts on some aspects of contemporary life and manners. Ordinary history examines a past age through a long-distance telescope. A book like this plants us in the midst of it, showing us everything in full detail and at life size. We have here a moving picture of how sixteenth century France dressed, ate and drank, talked, journeyed, made love, fell sick, died, and got buried. As a single illustration, we may take what he says on drinking in his day. His slap at the Teuton might be quoted in the present day as his countrymen's revenge for Sedan. "The Germans drink almost indifferently of all wines with delight; their business is to pour down and not to taste; and it's so much the better for them; their pleasure is so much the more plentiful and nearer at hand." In France he notes a decided abatement of drinking from the custom of the previous generation. The six-bottle men seemed dying out. "Is it," says he, "that we pretend to a reformation? Truly, no; but it may be we are more addicted to Venus than our fathers were." In the essay on the "Art of Conference," he, in a manner which strongly reminds us of a similar passage in Lucian, lashes into the pedantic humbugs of his time, who chattered the jargon of the schools without possessing a particle of common sense. His attack on the medical tribe in " The Resemblance of Children to their Parents," is an amusing revelation of the methods of the Faculty in his day. He ends it by an eulogium of their personal character, but with a firm refusal to swallow their prescriptions. Lastly, the essays have been the favourite book for writers and speakers from the fact that they are a perfect Golconda of classical illustration. Every page teems with apt quotations which the modern world has requisitioned wholesale, and without acknowledgment, for its articles and speeches. Altogether Montaigne must be pronounced indispensable. We may abuse him for his coarseness, for his scepticism, for his absence of ideal. It will nevertheless remain that there are very few books in the world of which it can be said with the same truth as of this one that the study and mastery of it in itself constitute a liberal education.

BOETHIUS.

OF the few names that shine upon the further edge of the Dark Ages there are none, whether in history or literature, more worthy of remembrance than that of Boethius. From the end of the nineteenth century to the beginning of the sixth is, it is true, "a far cry," and it is possible that the average British Philistine will aver that the problems of the former are quite enough for him, without raking up those of an age which might by this time be left comfortably to its slumbers. Others, however, will think differently; and hold, as we do, that the earlier time has a good many messages for the later. That age was a great and stirring one, critical in the history of the world. It was the age of Justinian and of Theodoric, of Belisarius and of Narses. It was the period when society, affrighted, beheld the great Roman Empire cracking to pieces before its eyes; when the imperial city had seen Alaric the Goth in its Senate House; when Europe had become a cauldron seething with new forces and new races, which were finally to shape themselves into the nations of the modern world. Theodoric, the Ostro-Goth, had waded through blood to the sovereignty of Italy. Once on its throne the barbarian chief, by a government so vigorous and far-seeing as to put him among the foremost rank of administrators, gave the land a long period of peace and of marvellous prosperity.

. Of his counsellors Boethius was for many years a leading figure. Of an illustrious Roman family he was by temperament a scholar and a philosopher. In him almost alone of his contemporaries the ancient Greek learning still survived. He was the translator of Pythagoras, of Euclid, of Ptolemy, and above all, of Aristotle.

But it is not upon these works that his fame rests. He lives for after ages in the contribution which he made to the pathetic roll of the literature of captivity. Literature is deeply indebted to prison walls. From under their shadow come some of St. Paul's noblest utterances. The immortal dreamer of Bedford wrote his " Pilgrim's Progress " as he lay " in a certain den." And the work of Boethius, which we always associate with his name, is the cry of " a spirit in prison." How he came there needs not much telling. A desire to re-establish the dignity of the Senate, and to

bring back some of the old Roman independence, excited the jealousy of his barbarian
master. On the testimony, as he avers and as
others also affirm, of false witnesses, he was
condemned and cast into prison, and in the end
put to death. It was in those weary months
when, stripped of all his honours and dignities,
he waited for the end, that his mind sought
relief from its anguish in lofty philosophic
contemplation. The result was the "*De Consolatione Philosophiæ*" with which he is for
ever identified.

This remarkable work is divided into five
books, and is written partly in prose and partly
in verse. It takes the form of a dialogue
between himself and Philosophy, who appears
to him in a vision in the form of a beautiful
woman. She reproaches him for his gloom and
depression, and proposes to cure him of his
sorrows. As a beginning she seeks to console
him by the reflection that true happiness lies,
after all, in the man himself and not in the
gifts of fortune. She appraises the value of
what men ordinarily seek after. Wealth is
nothing in itself, only in what it can purchase.
What is the value of power, since it is constantly being gained by the vilest; or of fame,
when we consider the narrowness of its range,
and the shortness of its duration? Fortune's
frown is often her best gift in leading us to the

contemplation of the only Good. Then comes
a disquisition on the nature of the supreme
Good, which is found to reside only in God.
Boethius here asks a question which has tor-
mented the ages, and over which Mill stumbled
—How can we believe in an all-powerful and
all-beneficent Deity, and yet admit the existence
of evil? We get in answer some arguments
more subtle than satisfying. The wicked, we
are told, are always powerless, even when seeming to conquer, for they never obtain what they
seek. They seek the Good, but never get it
because they seek in the wrong way. They
cannot be said really to exist, for they have
violated the law of their nature, and become,
therefore, no longer men, but mere bodies.
There will come an end to evil by its natural
powerlessness.

Next are discussed the questions of Fate and
Providence, which are resolved into forms of
the Divine Will, which secures that nothing
happens by chance. The fifth book is taken
up with an elaborate discussion of Free Will
in its relation to the Divine Foreknowledge.
Does not the latter make the former impossible?
We get here a distinction drawn which later
theologians, such as Maurice, have so much
insisted on, between the idea of eternity and
that of mere perpetuity. Eternity, as implying
the whole and complete possession of all exist-

ence, can be predicated only of God. He includes in one act of perception all that was, is, and is to come. And as our seeing a man walking does not constrain him to continue or stop walking, so God's foreknowledge does not necessitate the act it contemplates. Boethius does not here touch the question so often dealt with by later thinkers, of the possibility of God limiting voluntarily His own omnipotence by the creation of beings endowed with free will. The book ends with the assurance that while God is omniscient, man also is free. It is not in vain that we lay our hopes and prayers before God. Though free, a strong necessity binds us to live uprightly, for otherwise we thwart ourselves, seeing that all our actions take place before the eyes of a Judge who seeth all things.

The book of which we offer this meagre outline has given rise to a controversy which has been the crux of scholars ever since. What was the relation of Boethius to Christianity? If it stood by itself the "*De Consolatione*" would be classed with the "*De Senectute*," or the "*De Natura Deorum*," rather than with works of a definitely Christian inspiration. Its doctrine of God, of Creation, of Sin, and of the Soul savour rather of the Porch, or the Academy, than of Palestine. Is Boethius to be taken, then, not only as he has been often called, "the last of the Romans," but also as "the last of the Pagans"? The question is singularly complicated by the existence of some other writings, which tradition unanimously ascribes to Boethius, and which are a direct pronouncement in favour of the orthodox faith. One of these, the " *De Trinitate*," follows the lines of Augustine's famous work, and another, " *Contra Eutychen et Nestorium*," refutes the Eutychian and Nestorian heresies on the person of Christ. Various have been the hypotheses to account for the discrepancy between the " *De Consolatione* " and the theological tracts. Some have roundly refused to accept the latter as authentic. But these, with the exception of the " *De Fide Catholica*," seem too firmly established by the consent of antiquity to be thus set aside. Others have adopted the device—a favourite one of both ancient and modern times—of making our author's book a Christian one by reading a Christian meaning into it. As some divines have found all the doctrines of St. Paul in the Book of Ecclesiastes, so commentators on the old Roman have proved that he was preaching orthodox Christianity, only in an emblematical way. Others, again, have formed the idea that the five books we possess are only an introduction to what Boethius really meant to say. If he had had time he would have advanced from philosophy to the higher consolations of revealed religion. The objection to this is that we get no satisfactory evidence of any such intention from anything the writer actually says.

To us the problem seems solvable by a very simple hypothesis, but one which critics generally appear to have overlooked. It is that of explaining Boethius on the supposition that, while a Christian by profession, he was by temperament and mental habitude mainly a philosopher and a classicist. It is to be observed that the tracts of Boethius, while dealing with subjects of Christian theology, are, in style and tone, purely philosophical. The topics were such as gave scope to his skill in dialectic, and it was natural that in a world which by this time had become professedly Christian, he should discuss subjects which were of such general interest. At the same time he was a man who, more than any other of his age, had imbibed the spirit of the great Greek and Roman poets and thinkers. His scholarly tastes had made him live in their world. And now that in his confinement and disgrace he is thrown in upon himself, he falls back on the line of thinking in which he is most at home. His case is by no means without parallel. The Renaissance shows us multitudes of men, in Italy and France especially, ecclesiastics by pro-

fession, who on occasion delivered themselves
duly in defence of orthodoxy, but whose tastes
and sympathies were essentially pagan. There
was, though, this difference between them and
Boethius. While the latter assimilated what
was best and noblest in the old world, too many
of the former revelled in the aspects of it which
were sensuous and base.

The influence of Boethius on after-literature
was very considerable, though not what some
of his admirers have been fond of asserting. As
a director of the course of thought during the
Middle Ages he is not, as a philosopher even, to
be for one moment compared with Augustine.
The great Churchman in all departments of
serious thinking reigned without a real rival for
a thousand years. Not a thinker of any note,
from Cassiodorus to Descartes, fails to show
his indebtedness to the Bishop of Hippo. It
would be absurd to contend that the same may
be said of Boethius. Not the less is he to be
regarded as a deeply-interesting figure, and his
great work to be had in remembrance. He
marks an epoch. He was almost the last on
the farther side of the Middle Ages in whom
shone the light of the old Greek civilisation.
He was a far nobler representative of it than
Lucian. Rather was he worthy to be named
with Hypatia. After his death the gloom of
the Dark Ages settled into deeper blackness,

and many centuries were to roll away ere the lamp of culture, once more held aloft, brought again to light the treasures of the intellectual aristocracy which had taught and sung by the shores of the Ægean.

OUR NATIONAL LITERATURE.*

Mr. Churton Collins, in his new book, pre--
sents a very vigorous manifesto on the claims
of English Literature as a subject of University
teaching. He is anxious to secure three things :
first, the establishment of an English Literature
School at Oxford and Cambridge, capable of
conferring a degree in Honours of the same
value as one in Philosophy, Mathematics, or
Divinity ; secondly, that this study shall not,
as is now the case, be confounded with, or
made subordinate to, that of Philology ; and,
thirdly, that it shall, at the University, be
vitally related to that of the Greek and Latin
classics, and to the literatures of France and
Italy, as necessary to its proper comprehension
and appreciation. Mr. Collins has contrived
very cleverly to ally his specialty to what some
are disposed to call the almost lost cause of the
dead languages. He is almost as great an
enthusiast for the literature of Greece and Rome.
as for that of his own land, and in endeavouring

* The Study of English Literature. By John
Churton Collins. Macmillan and Co.

to prove that we must know the former in order
to understand the latter he is neatly killing two
birds with one stone. We shall have a word to
say on this point presently. Meanwhile it is
to be observed that the question of the study
of our national literature may be discussed
from two points of view. The scheme which
Mr. Churton Collins is urging deals with the
supply and training of University teachers of
the subject. Bnt there is also the consideration of this study on the part of the general
educated public. The manner in which the
English public of to-day regards its own literature is influenced by two considerations which
ought not to be overlooked.

The first is, that our national literature is
not, strictly speaking, our sacred literature.
With the Jews, the Greeks, and other early
peoples, the national writings were valued, and
were made the chief instrument of intellectual
and moral culture, for the reason that they
formed, not simply a literature, but the record
and embodiment of their religion. Their
literature was, at the same time, their theology.
It has been otherwise with us. Our purely
national literature, not being the authoritative
expression of our religious faith, has not secured
for its study, as did the Greek and the Jewish,
the front place in the list of intellectual and
moral duties. It is, at best, a *parergon*. Our

drama, our history, our poetry, are something
to envy and to be proud of; but they make no
claim to be religiously cultivated. A second
consideration is the competition of other literatures. With the vast extension of possible
studies, an extension which has been accom-
panied with a corresponding growth of other
interests and pursuits, the tendency of the
modern mind is perforce towards an eclectic
and a cosmopolitan rather than to national
cultivation of literature. The educated Englishman of to-day finds himself in front of an
enormous mass of reading, the product of many
ages and of many countries. His time is
limited, and he must make a selection. Out of
the myriad of books that are offered, some, he
finds, are in the first rank, as being the very
highest product of human genius. Of these
his own country has produced a certain proportion. For the rest he must go outside. For
the purposes of the highest possible culture he
feels it will be better for him to make his
principle of selection a search for the intrin-
sically best rather than a cult of the merely
national. In comedy he will very likely read
Molière in preference to the minor dramatists
of the Restoration. In philosophy, if he has
to choose, he will perhaps prefer Descartes to
the Cambridge Platonists. In thus declaring
that he prefers what is first-rate, though it be

foreign, to what is twelfth-rate, though it be English, who is blame him?

At this point, however, we find ourselves grievously in need of a definition. What, after all, is English literature? Is the Bible English literature? The majority of people would say that the Authorised Version, representing as it does the strength, the majesty, and the simplicity of the style of the Elizabethan age, is as much an English classic as are Hamlet or the "Canterbury Tales." If we admit that, we at once open the whole question of translations. Is Pope's "Homer" English literature, in the same way as his "Rape of the Lock"? When the student has mastered Jowett's "Plato," has he acquainted himself with an English as well as a Greek classic? We are disposed to say "yes," and to add that, if we can get the best minds of a generation to stir themselves, not only to original production, but to securing to their country works which, as to their substance, shall be the masterpieces of other languages, and as to their form masterpieces of their own, we shall get by this means for the general public a literature which will be an adequate instrument of culture without going outside.

We are not here, let it be well understood, for a moment arguing that a man can get out of the best translation all that he will find in the original.: To a classical scholar the charms of Horace and of Homer lie as much in the music of their syllables as in the sense of the words.. Is " Ocean's unreckonable laughter " the same as κυμάτων ἀνήριθμον γέλασμα? Are we satisfied with "the many-sounding sea" as an equivalent for πολυφλοισβοίῳ Θαλάσσης? The one says to us something about the sea; the other makes us behold it rippling in the sunlight, and then filling our ears with its roar upon the beach. But the fact is that, of the actual public which spends a good proportion of its school-time in getting a smattering of Latin and Greek, nine-tenths never obtain enough to even understand, far less enjoy, an author who writes in these languages. They are floundering in a mire of prepositions and particles instead of communing joyfully with the mind of their poet or historian. Their only chance of a culture which shall comprehend the great thinkers and singers of the past is in making the study of English literature to include that of translations of the masterpieces. And the translations in their form ought to be not less than masterpieces.

Admitting this, we are not the less decidedly with Mr. Collins in his contention that no one has any business to attempt the teaching or profession of English literature in any serious fashion who has not as a qualification a com-

14

petent knowledge of the Greek and Latin classics as well as of the great European literatures. Hegel has taught us that to know a thing we must know something else; in other words, we cannot comprehend anything apart from its relations. Now the Classics are related to English literature as the soil is to the tree which grows in it. And that is true of our literature all along the line. Our earlier authors make it more manifest by the quotations with which they crowd their pages. But our later writers, though they have largely dropped this habit, require not the less a knowledge of the Classics to properly understand and appreciate them. Chaucer is not more intimately related to Boccaccio than is Wordsworth to Plato; or than Macaulay, as to his form, to the Thucydides with whom he cared only to be compared. And it is only by this outside knowledge that a teacher could secure to his pupils the intellectual pleasure which comes from studying a great work in the company of its intellectual kinsmen. For a man to expound "Macbeth" without a knowledge of the "Agamemnon" would be as meagre a performance as to lecture on Modern Painters without knowing anything of Van Eyck or Da Vinci.

Not the less evident is it that an acquaintance with the literature of the Continent is as necessary to a really thorough academical knowledge of English as is a training in the Classics. A French professor of literature would be entirely at sea who should attempt to explain the Romanticism of the first half of this century in France apart from any study of Sir Walter Scott. But so equally would an English teacher who proposed to expound Dryden or Pope apart from any reference to French classicism. And if French is wanted, so is Italian. The relation of the Renaissance literature of Italy to our own—the way in which Dante, Ariosto, Petrarch, and Boccaccio wrought both on the spirit and form of our writers in the great age which begins with Chaucer and ends with Milton—is too obvious to require any dwelling upon.

It is evident then, from considerations of this sort, that a school of English literature at our Universities is needed, and that it should have an adequate programme. Our teaching of this subject needs to be properly organised, and it is the business of the Universities to take this in hand. We are badly in want of a standard both of method and of qualification. At present there is neither. A man may teach anything : he may give a philological disquisition on Anglo-Saxon, or string together simply a long list of names and dates, or offer a general gaol delivery of all the pamphleteers and tenth-rate scribblers of some obscure and limited period, and call this exercise a course of English literature. The subject deserves a better fate. We trust we shall not have much longer to wait for an arrangement at our Universities which shall secure the equipment, for the purposes of our national secondary education, as well as in the interests of sound criticism, of a race of teachers who will know how to deal with both the genesis and the genius of our literature, and to accurately estimate the position it occupies in the intellectual movement of the world.

www.ingramcontent.com/pod-product-compliance
Lightning Source LLC
Chambersburg PA
CBHW030130030726
47498CB00007B/2628